"Me and My Big Mouth!"
Study Guide

by
Joyce Meyer

NEW YORK   BOSTON   NASHVILLE

FaithWords
Copyright © 2001 by Joyce Meyer
Life In The Word, Inc.
P.O. Box 655
Fenton, Missouri 63026
All rights reserved. Except as permitted under the U.S. Copyright Act of 1976, no part of this publication may be reproduced, distributed, or transmitted in any form or by any means, or stored in a database or retrieval system, without the prior written permission of the publisher.

FaithWords
Hachette Book Group USA
237 Park Avenue
New York, NY 10017
Visit our Web site at www.faithwords.com

Printed in the United States of America

First FaithWords Edition: October 2002
10 9 8 7 6 5

FaithWords is a division of hachette Book Group USA, Inc.
The FaithWords name and logo is a trademark of Hachette Book Group USA, Inc.

ISBN 978-0-446-69106-2
LCCN: 2002110911

Contents

Introduction

Words are containers for power. They have the power to be either creative or destructive. Every day we have new opportunities to say words that encourage, edify, and give hope. What we say to or about others as well as ourselves can gloriously heal or deeply hurt.

You may not realize that right speaking follows right thinking — thinking thoughts in line with the Word of God.

Our words come directly from our thoughts or mind, a part of our soul. As defined in this study, the soul consists of the mind or intellect, the will, and the emotions or feelings. We who have a personal relationship with Jesus through believing in Him have the mind of Christ, according to 1 Corinthians 2:16. This means that we hold the thoughts, feelings, and purposes of His heart. But when we operate by what *we* feel, think, or want according to the desires of our flesh, or "sinful nature" (Galatians 6:8 NIV), we're not thinking like Jesus thinks, and we say things we shouldn't say.

What we express through our mouths as what we want, think, and feel may not be in agreement with what God wants for us. We can reach the point of feeling that what we say is out of control — we say things for which we are immediately sorry. Even we believers can have a problem taming our tongue when we do not have right thinking. There is a continual struggle between the flesh and spirit. Instead of submitting to the desires of the flesh, with the help of the Holy Spirit we can learn to think God's thoughts. And as we continue to choose to submit to the Holy Spirit, eventually our desires are changed into God's desires, and our speech will begin to reflect God's heart more and more.

It is possible to master the mouth!

If your words are not producing the kinds of results or effects you want or expect and your mouth is giving expression to the wrong mindset, with the help of the Holy Spirit you can learn how to engage in uplifting conversation and purposely order what you say. The mouth can be trained to stop speaking out of the mind, feelings, and fear, but it is a process that requires time and persistence.

As you begin working in this study guide, I believe that the importance of your words will become clear to you, and you will move forward toward gaining control of your mouth. You can be saved from the destructive power of your own words. Learning how to bring your words under control will bring positive results in your life and circumstances. And when that happens, it will bless the lives of everyone around you.

Using This Study Guide

The purpose of this workbook is to reinforce the principles taught in my book, *"Me and My Big Mouth!"* You will need a copy of *"Me and My Big Mouth!"* to work through this book.

This study guide is written in a question and answer format. By reading a chapter in *"Me and My Big Mouth!"*, studying the designated Scripture verses, and answering the questions in the corresponding chapter of the study guide, you will gain a deeper understanding of the principles and learn more easily how to incorporate them into your daily life.

To use this workbook, look up and read the corresponding chapter in *"Me and My Big Mouth!"* Next look up in your Bible the Scriptures designated in the study guide and read them. This is an important step because those Scriptures are the basis of the teaching in that particular chapter and are taken directly from that chapter.

Answer the questions in the study guide by referring to the appropriate chapter in *"Me and My Big Mouth!"* Once you have finished answering the questions in each chapter, turn to the answer key in the back of this book to check your answers.

1. Work at a comfortable pace. Don't rush to finish quickly. Stay in each chapter until you have a thorough understanding of the material and how it pertains to your life.

2. Follow these steps with each chapter in this study guide.

3. Use this study guide for individual study or group discussion. When using it in a group, discuss your answers and learn how to apply the principles in a way that may not have occurred to you until you heard the experiences of others.

Consistently and steadily working through this book will help you gradually transform your mouth into verbalizing God's Word instead of expressing the wrong, negative words of the enemy, Satan. Changing your way of speaking will enable you to change things in your life that you thought you would have to live with forever. As you agree with God through your words, you will begin to experience His best for you.

MAKE YOUR WORDS WORK FOR YOU

Proverbs 18:21 states, "Death and life are in the power of the tongue, and they who indulge in it shall eat the fruit of it [for death or life]." No subject mentioned in the Bible should be taken more seriously than the mouth. By gaining control of our words, we are making a vital move toward living in God's good plan for our life.

You may be struggling with a mouth that seems to have a mind of its own, but that can change. It is my sincere prayer that this study guide will help you to control the words you speak and make them work for you.

God bless you as you take the first step toward mastering your mouth and becoming a mouthpiece for the Lord.

1. As defined in this study, what does the soul consist of?_____
   _____
   _____.

2. Read 2 Timothy 2:21

   Why can and should the soul be purified and rendered a vessel fit for the Master's use? _____
   _____.

3. a. To what does our mouth give expression? _____
      _____
      _____.

   b. What does our mind tell us? _____
      _____
      _____.

   c. What does our will tell us?_____
      _____
      _____.

d. What do our emotions tell us?_____

_____

_____.

4. What happens as our soul is purified?_____

_____

_____

_____.

5. Read 1 Corinthians 2:16

What does the Word of God teach us in this passage? _____

_____

_____

_____.

6. What makes up what the Bible refers to as "the flesh"? _____

_____

_____.

7. Feelings can be trained to _____

_____,

but this is a process that _____

_____

_____.

8. To what does the mouth give expression? _____

_____

_____

_____

_____.

9. Review Proverbs 18:21

    Complete this Scripture: " _____
    and _____ are in the power of the tongue,
    and they who indulge in it shall _____
    _____
    _____."

10. Why should we take the subject of the mouth as seriously as any
    subject in the Bible? _____
    _____
    _____
    _____
    _____.

Learning to Speak God's Language

*I*n the original book, "Me and My Big Mouth!", read chapter 1, then read in your Bible the Scriptures designated below, and answer the questions that follow. When you finish, check your answers in the answer key provided at the end of this book.

   As you continue to follow this procedure throughout this workbook, you can be assured that you will gain insight through understanding that will help you integrate these godly principles into your daily life and win the battle to master your mouth!

1.   Read Mark 11:22,23; Luke 4:1-13

   a.   As we see in Mark 11:22,23, what does God's Word instruct us to do when we have mountains in our lives?_____
   _____.

   b.   When we speak to the mountains, what are we to hurl at them? Why? _____
   _____
   _____.

   c.   When tempted by Satan in the wilderness, according to Luke 4:1-13, how did Jesus answer every trial? _____
   _____
   _____
   _____
   _____.

d. What happens when we "try" this for a while, and then do not see quick results? _____

_____

_____

_____

_____.

e. Persistence is a vital link to victory. We must _____

_____

_____

_____.

2. Read Mark 11:24-26

a. What will happen if a person living in disobedience thinks he can speak God's Word to his mountains and get results?____

_____

_____.

b. There is no power in speaking to a mountain if the heart is full of _____.

c. Into what deception do multitudes of people fall who have accepted Christ as their personal Savior? _____

_____

_____

_____.

d. The central theme of the Bible is _____.

e. For many of us, our life is in a mess due to disobedience. The disobedience may have been the result of ignorance or rebellion, but the only way out of the mess is _____ _____ _____.

3. Read Deuteronomy 28:1,2; 1 Corinthians 1:9,10

a. As emphasized in these passages, what two things do we often choose to ignore in the Bible? _____ _____.

b. In 1 Corinthians 1:9 we see that God is faithful. How do we draw upon His faithfulness? _____ _____ _____.

c. Our disobedience does not change God's faithfulness. But obedience _____ _____ _____ _____.

4. Read 1 Corinthians 3:1

When we receive Jesus as our Savior, we enter into the new life of a believer. In this passage, the Apostle Paul tells us that as "babies in Christ," we simply do not know how to talk yet. Just as natural babies must learn to speak the language of their elders, so Christians must learn _____ _____.

5. Read Hebrews 5:13,14

    a. Although many things are clearly defined in the Word, and it is obvious what God's will is, in order to make decisions about things that are not spelled out in black and white, we need to _____

    _____.

    b. It takes _____ to know God, to know our own hearts, and to be able to be totally honest with ourselves and with God.

6. Read James 4:2,3,15,16; 1 Timothy 2:3,4; Proverbs 3:7

    a. _____ is a good example of something in the Word of God that is so clear that we never have to pray, "if it be Thy will."

    b. According to James 4:3, sometimes we ask God for something and yet fail to receive it because _____

    _____

    _____.

    c. If what we are asking for is not clearly spelled out in the Word, and we are not positive that we have heard from God about the issue, what is a wise and submissive way to pray?_____

    _____.

    d. What happens if the difference between faith and confidence, and foolishness and presumption is not discerned? _____

    _____

    _____.

e. We do not know anything at all, at least not compared to what God knows. We must resist the temptation to play "Holy Ghost, Jr." Instead, we must _____

_____.

7. Read Proverbs 13:16; 1 Peter 5:8; Proverbs 1:1-4

a. _____ are actually the devil's playground.

b. If the devil cannot get a believer to totally ignore a truth and live in deception, his next tactic will be _____

_____

_____

_____

_____.

c. _____ is a central theme of God's Word.

d. *Webster's II New College Dictionary* defines "wisdom" as _____

_____

_____

_____.

e. Wisdom does not operate in extremes. Proverbs 1:1-4 says that wisdom is full of _____, and

_____

_____.

f. Webster's defines "prudent," the adjective form of prudence, as _____

_____

_____.

g. What might we say that "wisdom" is? _____
_____
_____.

h. The statement that "you can have what you say" means you
can have what you say *if* what you say _____
_____
_____
_____.

i. What happens when you learn to cooperate with the Holy
Spirit?_____
_____
_____.

The Effect of Words in the Natural Realm

Chapter

2

As with the previous chapter, before answering the questions below, first read the corresponding chapter in "Me and My Big Mouth!" then the Scriptures designated below. After you complete the chapter, check the answer key in the back of this book.

To gain the greatest benefit from this workbook, continue using this method throughout.

1.   Read Romans 10:9,10

    a. In this passage, the Apostle Paul sets forth a spiritual truth applied to salvation, a truth that may be applied to other issues as well. What two things does the confession of a person's belief confirm? _____

        _____

        _____.

    b. What does a believer's confession declare?_____

        _____

        _____.

    c. How did the late biblical scholar W. E. Vine define two of the Greek words translated "confirm" in the *King James Version?*

        _____

        _____

        _____

        _____

        _____.

    d. How did W. E. Vine define the Greek word translated "confirmation"? _____.

    e. Based on these definitions, what does confession do for salvation?_____

        _____.

2.   Read Psalm 2:7

    a. What is God's formal decree? _____

       _____.

    b. What happens when a believer declares the Word out of his own mouth, with a heart full of faith? _____

       _____

       _____.

    c. When the Royal Decree is pronounced_____

       _____!

3.   Read Psalm 139:13-16; Jeremiah 29:11; review Romans 10:9,10

    a. According to the passage in Psalm 139, God's plan for our lives _____

       _____

       _____.

    b. According to Jeremiah 29:11, what kind of thoughts does God have toward us? What is their purpose? _____

       _____

       _____.

c. God has written down His will, His Word, for our lives. What happens as we believe it and speak it out loud for our lives?

_____

_____.

d. The reason some people see very little manifestation of the things they are believing for may be because they are believing but not speaking. Based on the passage in Romans 10:9,10, they would experience radical results if they would

_____

_____.

e. Some people are trying to live in the blessings of God while still _____.

f. What happens if we speak negative things? _____

_____.

g. We should remember that what we are speaking, we are

_____

_____

_____.

h. With our words, what can we draw out of Satan's realm?

_____.

i. What can we draw out of God's realm with our words?

_____.

4. Read Hebrews 1:3; 11:3; Genesis 1:26,27

a. These passages in the book of Hebrews tell us that the universe was created and upheld by_____

_____.

b. How does that fact relate to us? _____

_____

_____

_____.

5. Read Ephesians 5:1; Romans 4:17

As imitators of God, how are we to follow His example? _____

_____

_____

_____.

6. Read 1 Corinthians 9:19-22; 1 Corinthians 11:1;
Galatians 5:22,23; 1 Corinthians 13:5; Galatians 5:6;
1 Corinthians 2:14; Colossians 4:5,6

a. In the passage in 1 Corinthians 9:19-22, the Apostle Paul said
that he met people where they were in order to _____

_____.

b. According to 1 Corinthians 11:1, Paul told believers to imi-
tate him. That is especially important when dealing with
"those without"_____

_____.

c. In our conversations with others, we need to show them the
fruit of the Spirit — especially _____

_____ which

Paul tells us_____

_____.

d. How does faith work? _____.

e. The truth is that Jesus is our Healer, and truth is more powerful than _____.

f. How can we be imitators of God in calling "those things which be not as though they were" (Romans 4:17 KJV), and yet not be offensive to people who may not understand?

   _____

   _____

   _____

   _____

   _____

   _____

   _____.

g. In the passage in 1 Corinthians 2:14, we are told that the natural man does not accept the teachings and revelations of the Spirit "because they are _____ discerned."

h. In Colossians 4:5,6 Paul was saying to the believers of his day, and to us: "Be careful how you talk to those who are not on your level spiritually. Use _____ and _____. Be led by _____ _____."

Chapter 3

Calling Those Things That Are Not As Though They Are

1. Review Romans 4:17 KJV

   a. What is one of the greatest privileges we have as God's children? _____

   _____

   _____

   _____.

   b. This practice in Romans 4:17 KJV can work against us if we are calling for things that are not God's will but the enemy's (Satan). Some people fear what has not yet taken place, and by their negative faith they are _____

   _____.

2. Read Psalm 116:10; Joshua 1:8; Psalm 119:148; 1:2

   a. What is it called when we confess the truth of God's Word?

   _____.

   b. Can we confess things that we cannot find chapter and verse for? _____

   _____

   _____

   _____.

   c. In the passage in Joshua 1:8, God instructed Joshua to meditate on His Word "day and night." Part of meditation is ___

   _____.

    d. What does confessing the Word of God do? _____

_____

_____.

3.   Read Genesis 15:1-6; 17:5,15,16

    a. Why did God change the names of Abram and Sarai? _____

_____

_____.

    b. What happened each time their new names were called?___

_____

_____

_____

_____.

    c. Each time their new names were called, *words* were being spoken into the atmosphere that were _____

_____

_____.

    d. Those words were beginning to_____

_____.

Now the words on the earth were_____

_____

_____.

4.   Review Genesis 15:1-6; read Romans 4:18-21; Amos 3:3

    a. What did Abram do when God told him he would have a son of his own through whom he would become the father of many nations?_____.

b. Like Abraham (or Abram), we will never receive a miracle unless_____

_____

_____.

c. Not only did Abraham and Sarah believe God, but the words of their mouths were being used_____

_____.

d. What does speaking in agreement with God's Word, His written Word, or a specific word He has given us, do? _____

_____

_____.

e. We cannot walk with God concerning His plan for our lives unless_____

_____.

5. Read Deuteronomy 30:19; Matthew 12:34

a. In light of the passage in Deuteronomy 30:19 that says to "choose life," in order to carry God's dreams for our lives, and the lives of others, we must be willing or choose to "conceive." In other words, we must be willing _____

_____

_____.

b. Why is believing the first important step to carrying out God's dream for our lives and the lives of others? _____

_____

_____.

c. To what do our mouths give expression? _____
   _____.

d. What do we draw to ourselves? _____
   _____.

e. If we keep our soul and mouth full of doubt, unbelief, fear, and every negative thing, what will happen? _____
   _____.

f. If we keep our soul and mouth full of God and His Word and plan, what will happen?_____
   _____.

g. Whose choice is it about what will be drawn to us? _____
   _____.

Chapter
4

Prophesy Your Future

1. Read James 3:2; Matthew 12:37

    a. According to James 3:2, when does someone become ". . . a fully developed character and a perfect man. . . ."?_____

    _____

    _____

    _____.

    b. In Matthew 12:37, what did Jesus warn us about words?____

    _____

    _____

    _____

    _____

    _____

    _____.

2. Read James 3:4-8; John 8:44; Matthew 17:20

    a. According to James 3:4-8, can man tame the tongue?_____

    _____.

    b. Describe an undisciplined tongue. _____

    _____

    _____.

    c. What do we need to control our tongues? _____

    _____

    _____.

d. What else must we do to control our tongues? _____

_____

_____

_____.

e. You change things in your life by _____

_____

_____.

f. Can we curse our future? _____. If so, how?_____

_____.

Can we bless it? _____. If so, how? _____

_____.

g. When we curse our future with our words, when we agree with the devil instead of with God, we are *deceived*. What is deception?_____

_____.

h. Satan is called the deceiver because, as Jesus said in John 8:44, ". . . he is a_____

_____."

i. How does Satan try to deceive us? _____

_____

_____

_____.

3. Read Isaiah 65:16-18 KJV; 43:18,19

a. What twofold principle can be carried into every area in which we desire victory? _____

_____
_____
_____
_____.

   b. How can we release the plan of God for our lives? _____

_____
_____
_____
_____.

   c. If we stop mentally living in the past, we can _____

_____.

Once we do that, we can _____

_____. By so doing we can

_____.

4.   Read Matthew 12:36; review Proverbs 18:21

   a. Why did Jesus teach that men will one day have to give an account for their words? _____

_____
_____.

   b. What does Proverbs 18:21 state about the tongue? _____

_____
_____.

   c. The careless words we speak in the heat of the moment may not mean much to us, but they definitely _____

_____.

5. Read John 6:63

    a. To whom should you first prophesy your future? _____
       _____.

    b. What should you speak out? _____
       _____
       _____
       _____
       _____.

6. Read Matthew 26:41

    a. Sometimes we are guilty of getting spiritually lazy and "put-
       ting up with the enemy's junk." In this passage of Scripture,
       Jesus' admonition to His disciples, "Watch and pray," should
       first be applied to our own lives. What must we do when
       Satan comes against us? _____
       _____.

    b. Come against Satan when he is trying to get a foothold, and
       _____.

7. Read Revelation 19:11-15; Hebrews 4:12; 2 Corinthians 10:4

    a. Mixing _____ and _____
       does not equal power in God's economy.

    b. What is the sharp sword coming forth from the mouth of
       Jesus as depicted in Revelation 9:11-15? _____
       _____.

   c. Where does the Word of God operate?_____
_____.

   d. The Word of God is a spiritual (unseen) weapon that _____
_____.

8.   Read Isaiah 46:9,10; Romans 8:37; Revelation 1:8

   a. In light of Romans 8:37 that says "we are more than conquerors," we can know before the battle ever begins that
_____.

   b. Prophesying our future is literally_____
_____
_____.

9.   Read Isaiah 48:3

   a. What is the basic principle of God's method of operation?
_____
_____.

   b. God operates on _____ that He has set in place, and we_____.

   c. How does the spiritual law of sowing and reaping apply to our words? _____
_____
_____.

10.   Read Isaiah 48:5-7

   a. In this passage, the Lord said that the things He desired to do were called into being by the prophetic word. That is what we are to do, to_____

_____

_____.

b. How can you prophesy without "standing in the office of prophet"? _____

_____

_____.

11. Read Isaiah 42:9; John 14:6; 12:26

   a. If you are tired of the old things and want some new things in your life, what should you do? _____

_____

_____.

   b. How can you avoid being the devil's mouthpiece? _____

_____

_____

_____.

   c. How can you follow Jesus' example, and what will be the result? _____

_____

_____

_____.

Chapter
5

Becoming God's Mouthpiece

1. Read Isaiah 55:11

   a. The prophets were a _____ for God. They spoke His Word to whatever God told them to speak to, and like this passage says, His Word accomplished what He pleased and purposed wherever He sent it.

   b. Those who desire to be used by God need to allow Him to deal with them concerning _____ _____.

2. Read Romans 12:6,7

   a. If you are a teacher of God's Word in any degree, remember: _____ _____.

   b. If we desire the words of our mouth to carry God's power, then _____ _____.

3. Read James 3:1,2; 1 Timothy 3:2

   a. In light of the passage in James chapter 3, it appears that God has a stricter guideline for those who are teachers of the Word. They are to follow Christ themselves and to show others_____ _____.

   b. The Apostle Paul wrote that spiritual leaders are to be self-controlled. What is one of the areas in which they are to exercise this fruit of the Spirit? _____

_____.

c. Those trained to be God's mouthpiece will frequently be used to bring _____ and _____ to others.

4. Read Proverbs 15:23; 25:11; Isaiah 50:4

a. According to Isaiah 50:4, why did the Lord God give the prophet a tongue of a disciple and of one who is taught?___

_____

_____.

b. These passages of Scripture are actually saying that we can bless people with _____

_____. We can

_____

_____.

c. If you have children, when they are hurting, what should you remember to speak to them? _____

_____

_____.

5. Read 1 Thessalonians 5:11; Romans 12:8; John 14:26

a. According to 1 Thessalonians 5:11, what are we to do for one another? _____

_____

_____.

b. What gift is spoken of in Romans 12:8? What is it? _____

_____

_____

_____.

c. In John 14:26, the Holy Spirit is called the _____. In this capacity, He _____

_____

_____

_____

_____.

d. You and I need to see and realize that exhortation is _____

_____ — _____.

e. As an exhorter, we can actually prevent someone from _____

_____!

f. How is the ministry of an exhorter compared to the ministry of the Holy Spirit as a "Comforter"? _____

_____

_____

_____

_____

_____

_____.

g. What were the early Christians instructed to do by the Apostle Paul in 1 Thessalonians 5:11? _____

_____.

h. Even if our ministry gift is not exhortation, we need to learn the importance of it and always try to remember that _____ _____ _____.

6. Read Ephesians 4:29; Romans 12:3; Isaiah 6:5

a. According to Ephesians 4:29, what kind of words are supposed to come out of our mouths? _____ _____ _____ _____ _____ _____ _____.

b. How did the Apostle Paul correct people? _____ _____ _____.

c. People who only want to correct but never edify, build up, exhort, or comfort are _____ _____.

d. God desires to touch more people's _____ and have them for His own _____ _____.

e. You are urged to allow God to deal with you in these very important areas, and like Isaiah, realize that _____ _____ _____.

Chapter
6

Complain and Remain,
Praise and Be Raised

1. Read John 6:43 KJV; review Ephesians 4:29; read Romans 12:21

   a. What is complaining? What's wrong with it? _____
   _____
   _____
   _____
   _____ .

   b. What else does complaining do? _____
   _____ .

   c. Words are containers of _____ .

   d. Why are complaining, grumbling words said to carry destructive power? _____
   _____
   _____
   _____ .

   e. What does God think of murmuring and complaining? Why?
   _____
   _____
   _____ .

   f. Why should we praise God rather than complain about what
   is going on right now? _____
   _____
   _____
   _____ .

    g. The best way to start every day is with_____

          _____ and_____.

    h. Why do truly thankful people not complain? _____

          _____

          _____

          _____

          _____.

    i. The world is full of two forces: _____

       and _____.

       The Bible teaches us that _____ overcomes

       _____

       _____.

    j. If we find ourselves faced with a negative (evil) situation, we

       can _____

       _____.

    k. Praise and thanksgiving are _____;

       complaining and grumbling are _____.

2.   Read Proverbs 14:30; 15:4

    a. How can words affect the physical body?_____

       _____

       _____.

    b. The tongue has _____.

    c. What effect does "willful contrariness," such as envy, jealousy, and wrath, have on the physical body? _____
_____.

    d. Praise and thanksgiving release_____
_____ and _____.

3.   Read 1 Corinthians 10:9-11

    a. When we complain, how does God react? Why? _____
_____
_____
_____
_____
_____.

    b. When we murmur, gripe, and complain, we are _____
_____
_____.

    c. Why was the Israelites' exploitation of God's goodness recorded in the Old Testament and recounted in the New Testament? How should it affect us?_____
_____
_____
_____
_____.

4.   Read Proverbs 21:23; 13:3; Deuteronomy 1:2; Hebrews 13:15 KJV

    a. These Scriptures verify that the person who _____
_____

but the person who _____
_____.

b. How were the wilderness experiences of the Israelites different from the wilderness experience of Jesus?_____

_____

_____

_____

_____

_____

_____

_____.

c. What lesson should we learn from these experiences? _____

_____

_____

_____

_____

_____.

d. We can _____,
   or _____.

5. Read Philippians 4:6

a. What is the antidote for the poison of complaining? _____

_____.

b. Complaining _____,
   whereas thanksgiving_____

_____.

c. Being thankful shows maturity. It demonstrates that we are

_____

_____

_____ .

d. How can being thankful also be a sacrifice? _____

_____

_____

_____

_____

_____

_____ .

6. Read Psalm 50:14; 107:21,22; 116:17

a. In Psalm 116:17 when did the psalmist say that he would call
    on the name of the Lord? _____

_____

_____ .

b. What kind of power is complaining filled with? _____

_____ .

7. Read Hebrews 13:15; Philippians 2:14; 1 Thessalonians 5:18;
    Ephesians 5:20

a. According to Hebrews 13:15, when are we to offer up to God
    a sacrifice of praise? _____

_____ .

b. The flesh looks for _____

_____, but the spirit searches for

_____.

c. From the Scriptures listed to read above, we see that not only
are we to avoid grumbling, faultfinding, complaining, ques-
tioning, and doubting, we are also to give thanks _____

_____, _____,

and _____.

d. We do not have to thank God _____
all the negative things in our life, but we are to give Him
thanks _____ them.

e. The praising life is the _____ life!

8. Read Ephesians 4:29-31

   a. To what is grieving the Holy Spirit connected? _____

   _____.

   b. Based on this passage, what does speaking evil include? ___

   _____

   _____

   _____.

9. Read Ephesians 5:4

   a. What Paul is telling us in this Scripture is, "Instead of vexing,
   offending, and saddening the Holy Spirit, _____

   _____."

b. The _____, _____,
   _____
   spirit absolutely must be eradicated from the Church.

c. _____
   only keep us right where we are; they prevent us from going
   forward with God.

d. _____are like weeds;
   if left unattended, they _____.

e. People with a critical spirit are _____
   to their problems.

f. Complaining is like _____
   _____. When we complain,
   we are calling for _____
   _____.

g. A critical spirit often is rooted in _____.

h. How do we stop complaining about what we do not have?

   _____
   _____
   _____
   _____.

i. We all have strengths and weaknesses, so if we are to have
   good relationships with one another, we must_____
   _____
   _____.

10. Read 2 Timothy 3:1,2

   a. Just as Paul predicted long ago in this passage of Scripture, we live in an _____ and _____ generation.

   b. The more others around us complain, the more we should _____.

11. Read Philippians 2:14,15; 2 Corinthians 3:2 KJV

   a. We should avoid complaining because it is _____ _____.

   b. According to 2 Corinthians 3:2 KJV, we are to be_____ _____.

   c. We don't need to show the world religion; we need to show them Jesus. How do we do that?_____ _____.

   d. Why are we commanded to be different from the world?

   _____
   _____.

12. Read Philippians 4:4-6 TLB

   a. You and I need to make it a daily challenge not to _____ _____ or _____ _____ with anything. What does that mean? _____ _____.

    b. When there is an attitude adjustment, then _____

        _____.

    c. Be generous in your gratitude, and it will _____

        _____.

13.   Read Psalm 133:1

    The devil wants us to have strife, arguing, upsets, etc. in our relationships. If he can get us to be negative, he can _____

    _____.

14.   Read Philippians 4:12; Zechariah 4:10

    a. As we see in these passages, we can learn how not to_____
        _____ during the kind of hard times
        that come to all of us, especially _____

        _____.

    b. We will never be "promoted" to better things if we do not

        _____.

    c. Complaining is sowing seeds also, but seeds that will produce

        _____.

        Sowing seeds of being thankful *in* — not *for* — the situation
        we face will produce_____

        _____.

15.   Read Hebrews 6:15; 1 Kings 18:44,45

    a. According to Hebrews 6:15, what was Isaac?_____

        _____.

b. In the passage in 1 Kings 18, what was the small cloud that Elijah saw? _____

_____.

16. Review Zechariah 4:10; read Hebrews 13:5; 12:2; Philippians 1:6; Hebrews 3:6

a. When we are believing God for something and we find evidence of a small beginning — a little seed, a cloud the size of a man's hand — why should we rejoice over our seed even though it is little? _____.

b. How do we curse that seed? _____

_____.

c. How do we plant that seed?_____

_____.

d. If we don't take care of the seed God gives us, we lose it. If we lose the seed,_____

_____.

e. Part of Hebrews 13:5 says, in essence, _____

_____.

f. How can we be content during the small beginning? Why?

_____

_____

_____

_____

_____

_____.

Cross Over to the Other Side

1. Read John 14:30; Isaiah 53:7

    a. When is one of the most difficult times for us to discipline our minds, mouths, moods, and attitudes? _____
    _____.

    b. We all experience the storms of life in varying degrees, we all have our faith tested and tried, and we all must learn how to
    _____.

    c. According to these passages, what did Jesus do when He was experiencing the most intense pressure? Why? _____
    _____
    _____
    _____
    _____
    _____.

    d. When faced with trying situations, what did Jesus purposely decide and declare He was going to do?_____
    _____.

    e. Instead of speaking out of upset emotions or wounded feelings during times of stress, it is always best to _____
    _____.

2. Read Mark 4:35

    When Jesus says to us, "Let's do a new thing," or, "Let's go over to the other side," or any variety of phrases He uses, He is communicating to us that_____

_____.

3.   Read Mark 4:37,38; review Romans 8:37

   a.   When God calls us to launch out to a new thing like He did to the disciples in Mark chapter 4, we leave the security of where we are and start out for the blessings of the other side. But it is often in _____

_____.

   b.   The middle is often a _____

_____.

   c.   Have you ever had times when you were in a storm and you prayed, you spent time with the Lord, you searched for an answer, but it seemed as though Jesus was asleep; the storm raged on and you didn't know what to do about it? We sometimes refer to those seasons as_____

_____ or _____

_____.

   d.   It is at times like this that we must_____

_____.

   e.   It is also at such times when we discover_____

_____.

   f.   Faith, like muscle, is strengthened by_____

_____, not by _____.

   g.   Each storm we go through_____

_____.

h. According to Romans 8:37, ". . . we are more than conquerors. . . ." That means that we _____
   _____.

i. Faith is for those times when we don't have the _____
   _____ yet. Faith is for the_____.

4. Read Mark 4:39,40

   a. In this passage, Jesus _____ the storm,
      but He _____ the disciples for their lack of faith.

   b. It is vital to our future that we _____
      _____
      _____.

   c. One of the things about us that has to change is our response
      to the storms of life. It is certain that we must _____
      _____
      _____.

5. Read Hebrews 10:23

   a. According to Hebrews 10:23 KJV, it is time for us to _____
      _____,and ride out the
      storms, knowing that _____
      _____
      _____.

   b. God is faithful, and we can hold to His hand during the
      storm, knowing that_____
      _____.

6. Read James 3:10,11

    a. In light of this passage of Scripture, we should strive to elimi-
        nate "double talk." What is "double talk"? _____

        _____

        _____.

    b. _____ of the tongue should be our goal.
        It is a sign of _____.
        It is one way we _____ God.

7. Read James 1:26

    a. According to this verse, we can do all types of good works,
        but if we do not bridle the tongue, they are all _____

        _____.

    b. How does Webster's define the word "bridle"? _____

        _____

        _____

        _____

        _____.

    c. What may happen if we don't bridle the tongue in the midst
        of the storms of life?_____

        _____.

    d. Who will be our bridle?_____

        _____

        _____.

8.   Read James 3:3-5

   a.   What do these Scriptures indicate about the tongue? What might one say about our words? _____

   _____

   _____

   _____.

   b.   How does Webster's define the word "bit"? _____

   _____

   _____

   _____.

   c.   We need a bit in our mouths, but it will not be forced on us; we must choose it. How will the Holy Spirit function as the bit if we choose His leadership? _____

   _____

   _____

   _____.

9.   Read Psalm 32:9

   a.   Our relationship with the Holy Spirit is the same as a horse being controlled by the pull of the bridle, which controls the bit in his mouth. The Holy Spirit is our _____.
   If we follow His promptings, what results will we get?_____

   _____

   _____.

   b.   What will happen if we don't follow Him?_____

   _____.

10. Read 2 Corinthians 10:5; Romans 12:1,2; Philippians 4:8;
     Psalm 19:14

     a. What is the root source of our words? _____
         _____.

     b. According to 2 Corinthians 10:5 KJV, what is the remedy for
         the problem of wrong thinking? _____
         _____
         _____
         _____
         _____.

     c. In light of Romans 12:1,2, what must happen to the mind in
         order to ever experience God's good plan?_____
         _____.

     d. Satan wants to control our mind. The Holy Spirit also wants
         to control our mind, but He never forces Himself on us. Who
         decides which one will get control? _____
         _____.

     e. According to Philippians 4:8, what things are we to think on?
         _____
         _____
         _____
         _____
         _____.

     f. In Psalm 19:14, why did the psalmist mention both the mind
         and the mouth? _____
         _____.

11.   Read Psalm 119:1; Deuteronomy 26:14; Mark 4:17; John 16:33

a. In light of Psalm 119:1, we must order our conversation in accordance with_____.

b. How should you see yourself and your circumstances in a time of trial? _____
_____.

c. Many people backslide during challenging times, and part of the reason they do so is because _____
_____.

d. It is harder to be obedient to the Lord during _____
_____.

e. Satan does not want you to get to the other side. He does not want you to make any progress at all. He wants to see you
_____
_____.

f. According to Mark 4:17, what happens to people who have no root in themselves? _____
_____
_____
_____
_____
_____
_____.

g. According to John 16:33, what has Jesus done for us? _____
_____.

12. Read Ezekiel 37:1-10

   a. As we see in this passage, God can totally revive and bring breath and spirit back into what was once only dead, dry bones. He can do the same for us, but not unless _____

   _____.

   b. We can no longer speak with _____

   _____and under pressure allow

   _____.

13. Read John 11:1-44

   a. In light of this passage, if Jesus can raise a dead man, surely He can raise a_____.

   b. We can see from the account of Lazarus in this passage that no matter how bad things seem, _____

   _____.

14. Read Mark 5:25-34

   a. What did the woman with the issue of blood do to receive her healing? _____.

   b. How was her faith released? _____

   _____.

   c. What is one way we activate our faith? _____

   _____.

   d. What should we do until we receive what we're believing for?

   _____.

15. Read Zechariah 9:12

    a. What does this verse mean when it refers to us as "prisoners of hope"? What is hope? _____

       _____

       _____

       _____

       _____.

    b. God is still God, and this Scripture tells us that if we will remain positive and be "prisoners of hope," He will _____

       _____

       _____.

16. Read Psalm 141:3; 17:3; 19:14

    a. Why do we need to pray Psalm 141:3, "Set a guard, O Lord, before my mouth; keep watch at the door of my lips," continually? _____

       _____

       _____.

    b. When we are crossing over to the other side and suddenly find ourselves in the middle of the journey with the storm raging, we will definitely have to _____

       _____.

    c. In light of Psalm 19:14, why should we pray the Word of God? _____

       _____

       _____

       _____.

d. What will be the result if you are sincere in your desire to gain victory in this area and seek God for His help?_____
_____
_____.

e. All those who follow God-ordained guidelines get _____
_____.

Is Your Mouth Saved?

1. Read Philippians 2:12; Ephesians 2:8,9

    a. It is not enough to be saved; the _____ must be saved also.

    b. That is part of the process which the Apostle Paul referred to in Philippians 2:12 as _____ _____ one's own salvation.

    c. God has freely given us salvation through His Son Jesus. Although it cannot be earned, it must be "worked out." This process is just another phase of our walk with the Lord. We might say that He _____

    _____

    _____

    _____

    _____.

2. Read Galatians 3:16 KJV

    a. How does the Bible refer to Jesus Christ in this verse? _____

    _____.

    b. That means that if we have a seed we can have a _____

    _____.

    c. Jesus is the Seed of _____

    _____.

d. Who plants this Seed in us? What must be done to it?_____

_____

_____.

e. What must be done to the ground that it is planted in? ____

_____

_____.

f. What is the ground in which this seed is planted? _____

_____.

g. How do we do the work of tending the seed? _____

_____

_____

_____.

h. What would happen if any of us would go back in our thinking to the beginning of our walk with God and take an inventory of all the things He has changed in us since then? ____

_____

_____

_____.

i. When God says, "It is time for your mouth to be saved," it is not just a little teaching from the Holy Spirit on the importance of words, but_____

_____.

3. Read Proverbs 8:6-8

This passage reveals the right way to use our mouth.

What did God have to do with three men (Jeremiah, Moses, and Isaiah) in the Bible who were called but who had a mouth problem? _____

_____

_____.

4. Read Jeremiah 1:4-10; John 8:28; 12:50

  a. God had called Jeremiah as a "prophet to the nations," but why did He have to straighten out Jeremiah's mouth before He could use Him? _____

  _____

  _____.

  b. Is this any different with us? _____.

  c. We need to say about ourselves_____

  _____.

  d. What did Jesus say about His speech? _____

  _____

  _____

  _____

  _____

  _____.

  e. God wants us to speak, not out of the _____,

    but out of the_____.

5. Read Jeremiah 5:14

  a. In this passage, God told Jeremiah that He would make His Word like fire in his mouth. In the past, Jeremiah may have been talking the way we talk now, but God was calling him up higher, to a new level. God is calling us in the same way, but on every new level of God's power and blessings we experience _____

_____ .

b. We must realize that wrong words can _____

_____ .

c. In order to have God's power, His anointing, released through our life, we cannot _____

_____

_____

_____ .

d. What usually happens when we ask God for something? _____

_____

_____

_____ .

e. Don't grieve over what has to go; _____

_____ .

6. Read Exodus 4:10-12

a. When God called Moses to be His spokesman to Pharaoh and the Israelites, what did Moses claim? _____

_____

_____ .

b. We think sometimes that God does not know about all of our weaknesses — but _____ .

    c. In Exodus 4:12 God answered Moses' doubt about his ability to speak to Pharaoh by telling him, _____

_____

_____

_____.

    d. The next time God tells you to speak for Him, and fear rises up within you, what should you do? _____

_____

_____.

7. Read Isaiah 6:1-9; 2 Timothy 2:21

    a. According to this passage, what does God need to do before He can use us? _____

_____.

    b. This Scripture passage teaches us that when we come into the presence of God,_____

_____.

    c. We all would prefer miracle deliverance from our "mouth problem," but often, the Lord has to _____

_____.

    d. Although Isaiah had an unclean mouth that was sinful and needed to be dealt with, what quality did he have that prompted God to choose him as His prophet?_____

_____

_____

_____.

e. What principle about what God is looking for when He calls us is set forth in these verses? _____

_____

_____

_____

_____

_____

_____.

f. God uses people who have flaws. He uses cracked pots! We come to Him as we are, and He_____

_____.

g. The _____, the _____, and the _____ are sometimes separate, even occurring in_____.

8. Read 1 Corinthians 3:11

a. In light of this passage, if you want to build the Kingdom of God, you must take time to_____

_____.

b. What is one of the first steps in laying that foundation? _____

_____.

9. Read John 8:32

a. What did Jeremiah, Moses, and Isaiah all realize that God had to change if they were to fulfill their divine call? _____

_____.

b. God will heal our mouths, but what must we do first?_____
   _____
   _____.

c. Jesus said that it is the truth that sets us free. The truth is that we need to say to the Lord, _____
   _____.

Fasting Includes Your Mouth

1. Read Isaiah 58:1-14

    Isaiah chapter 58 is a powerful portion of God's Word. What does it teach us? _____

    _____.

2. Review Isaiah 58:5

    a. True fasting is supposed to be for what purpose? What is it meant to be? _____

    _____

    _____

    _____

    _____

    _____.

    b. Are all people led to fast the same way? _____

    _____

    _____.

3. Review Isaiah 58:6

    a. According to this verse, what is the fast that God has chosen?

    _____

    _____

    _____.

    b. In order to set others free, what are we not supposed to do?

    _____

    _____.

    c. What do we need to do in order to break the yokes of bondage in our lives and the lives of those around us? Why?

_____

_____

_____.

4. Review Isaiah 58:7

    a. According to this verse, what else is part of the fast that God has chosen? _____

_____

_____

_____

_____.

    b. Whose needs are we to meet? _____

_____

_____.

5. Review Isaiah 58:8

In this chapter of Isaiah, there are many promises of peace and prosperity for us as God's people. What are they all dependent upon?

_____

_____.

6. Review Isaiah 58:9; read 2 Corinthians 5:20

    a. According to Isaiah 58:9, what things has God told us to do?

_____

_____
_____
_____
_____
_____.

b. In light of this passage in Isaiah 58, if our prayers are not being answered, it may well be because _____
_____
_____.

c. One of the things He has told us to do is to_____
_____
_____.

d. Another one of the things we are to do is to stop speaking
_____, _____,
_____, and _____.

e. The _King James Version_ of verse 9 translates the last phrase in that verse as "speaking vanity." What is vain speech?_____
_____
_____.

f. Being physically or mentally exhausted can be a sign of what?
_____.

g. In light of 2 Corinthians 5:20, as royal ambassadors, what are we required and expected to do?_____
_____
_____.

7. Review Isaiah 58:10-12

   a. When can you and I expect all the blessings of the Lord mentioned in this passage to come upon us and overtake us?

   _____

   _____

   _____.

   b. We must stop expecting God to pour out blessings on us while we _____

   _____.

8. Review Isaiah 58:11,13,14; read 2 Corinthians 2:14,15;
   Psalm 139:4; 19:14

   a. Basically, what is the Lord saying to us in Isaiah 58:13,14?

   _____

   _____

   _____

   _____

   _____

   _____

   _____

   _____

   _____.

   b. If you and I really want the blessing of God to be upon our lives, we have got to use our mouths _____

   _____

   _____.

c. We don't need to preach to people nearly as much as we need to _____

_____.

d. We don't need to "stir up a stink"; we need to_____

_____

_____.

e. How do we avoid being "stinky"?_____

_____

_____

_____

_____.

f. According to Psalm 139:4, Who knows every word that is still unuttered on our lips? _____.

g. That's why our prayer needs to be that of the psalmist, ____

_____

_____

_____

_____.

Chapter

10

The Slanderous Mouth

1. Review Proverbs 18:21

    a. What does Proverbs 18:21 mean? _____

    _____

    _____

    _____

    _____

    _____

    _____ .

    b. With this power we have the capacity for great _____

    _____ or great _____ ,

    for great _____ or great _____ .

    c. What can we use this power to create? _____

    _____

    _____

    _____ .

    d. How do we use this power? _____

    _____

    _____

    _____ .

    e. Who chooses how this power will be used? _____

    _____

    _____ .

2. Read Galatians 6:7,8 KJV; review Proverbs 18:21; read Ecclesiastes 5:1-7 TLB

    a. What spiritual principle from Galatians 6:7,8 KJV is recalled by the second part of Proverbs 18:21? _____

    _____

    _____.

    b. Where is the power to do something about your future located? _____

    _____.

    c. If there is any place in our life that we need to exercise discipline and self-control, it is in _____.

    d. What does the Bible say about talking too much?_____

    _____

    _____.

    e. What happens when we talk too much? Why? _____

    _____

    _____

    _____.

3. Review Isaiah 50:4; read James 1:19; Nehemiah 8:10

    a. In light of Isaiah 50:4, what do we need to train ourselves to do?_____

    _____.

b. What does James instruct us to do in James 1:19?_____

_____

_____.

c. What do you think would happen if we thought about what we were going to say before we said it? _____

_____.

d. Why did the prophet say that the Lord had given him the tongue of a disciple — a learner, one who is taught? _____

_____

_____.

e. According to the Bible, what is our strength? _____

_____.

f. Where are you and I as believers learning to find our joy? _____

_____.

g. While we are in the process of learning, what will keep us from growing weary? _____

_____.

4. Read James 3:8-10 KJV; 1 Timothy 3:11 KJV

a. What disturbs God about our mouth? _____

_____

_____

_____

_____.

b. What is one of the biggest favors we can do God and ourselves? _____

_____

_____.

c. Why is there nothing wrong with being less than perfect, *if* we have a perfect heart toward God? _____

_____

_____.

d. What is one definition of the word "slanderers"? _____

_____

_____

_____.

e. Is criticism spread only by telling something to ten other people? Why or why not? _____

_____

_____.

f. What does the translation of the word "slanderers" as *diabolos* ("Satan . . . false accuser, devil")[2] mean in our lives?

_____

_____

_____.

g. What is the reason God is revealing this message to all of us?

_____

_____

_____.

h. Too often people who have been slandered or criticized by others can't lay hold of the good things of God because

_____

_____

_____.

5. Read Colossians 3:21; Luke 4:18 KJV

a. All of us are products of our environment, of what we came from, of how we were raised. Thank God, Jesus opens those doors, and we can go free. He is the _____

_____

_____.

b. What will happen if you come to Jesus hurt and wounded?

_____

_____

_____

_____

_____.

c. What lesson is set forth in this passage in Colossians 3:21?

_____

_____.

6. Read Colossians 3:18,19; Ephesians 5:21

a. What do we see in Colossians 3:18,19? _____

_____

_____.

b. What are wives told to do as part of their calling in Christ Jesus? _____

_____.

c. It is not part of our nature to "adapt" to anyone else, but it is part of our _____

_____.

d. What are husbands told to do? What does this mean? _____

_____

_____

_____

_____.

e. What can wives and husbands do to be a "sweetheart" to each other? _____

_____.

7. Read Proverbs 18:14; review Romans 12:8

a. This verse is saying that regardless of what comes into a person's life, he can bear up under it if _____

_____

_____.

b. In Romans 12:8, what is one of the ministry gifts to the Church? _____

_____.

c. Why is it easy to recognize an encourager or exhorter? ____

_____

_____

_____

_____

_____

_____.

     d. What can you and I do even though we may not "stand in the office of encourager or exhorter"? _____

_____

_____

_____

_____

_____.

8.   Read 1 Samuel 30:6

     a. We all have times when we need to be encouraged by others, but sometimes it seems that there is no one to encourage us. Instead of getting angry and letting bitterness and resentment come in, what can we do at those times when we feel that nobody cares about us, that nobody appreciates us? _____

_____

_____

_____.

     b. God will send you the very person or people you need to uplift, encourage, and edify you. First, you _____; then second, you _____.

     c. Remember, the spiritual rule is: you reap what you sow. How do you reap encouragement?_____

_____.

     d. What happens when we encourage and exhort an individual?

_____

_____

_____

_____.

e. In the same way, the Holy Spirit, the Comforter, comes along-
    side us to _____, to _____
    _____, to _____,
    to_____.

f. We have a choice. We can either open our mouth and use it
    as *diabolos* to_____
    _____, or
    we can use it as *parakletos* to_____
    _____.

g. When we open our mouth, what comes out can either be ____
    _____ or _____.

Chapter 11

Angry and Impatient Words Lead to Trouble

1. Read Ephesians 4:31; Romans 12:16

    a. What descriptive words are used in Ephesians 4:31 to identify the things that get us into trouble? _____

    _____

    _____

    _____

    _____

    _____

    _____.

    b. Which of these things pose the biggest problem for you? ____

    _____

    _____

    _____

    _____.

    c. Do you and I have to have bad tempers or get mad every time something doesn't go our way? Why or why not? _____

    _____

    _____.

2. Review James 1:19

    a. James tells us to be _____ to hear, but _____ to speak, _____ to take offense, and _____ to get angry.

b. Of these, what is the most important — and often the hardest part? _____.

c. When we get mad, when we are caught in a situation we cannot change no matter what we do, that's when we need to learn _____.

d. When you are in such a situation, why is it useless and pointless to get mad, angry, impatient, in a rage, or to pitch a fit?

_____

_____.

3. Review Romans 12:16; Ephesians 4:31

a. According to the Apostle Paul in this passage, we can learn to be _____ and _____. We can also be _____ and _____.

b. What is the root cause of the things listed by Paul in Ephesians 4:31? _____

_____.

c. As Paul points out in Romans 12:16, we have such an inflated opinion of ourselves that we think _____

_____.

4. Read James 4:1-3

a. If we would admit it, we have a tremendous problem with _____. Why? _____

_____

_____.

b. What are the two main reasons people argue?_____

_____

_____

_____

_____.

c. When things don't go as we want them to, we need to just ___

_____

_____

_____

_____

_____.

d. What is the only thing that is going to maintain God's anointing? _____

_____.

5. Read 1 Corinthians 13:4,5; 15:31; review Matthew 12:34

a. How does the Word of God describe love in this passage? ____

_____

_____

_____

_____

_____

_____

_____

_____.

b. What is the solution to the problem of arguing?_____

_____.

c. We have got to learn to love peace and harmony. In light of 1 Corinthians 15:31, how are we to maintain them? _____

_____

_____.

d. Why do we start wars over petty things, trifles? _____

_____

_____

_____.

e. What is the solution to the problem of selfishness? _____

_____

_____

_____.

f. In this study, what choices is the Lord asking you and me to make, by the power of the Holy Spirit? _____

_____

_____

_____

_____

_____

_____.

6. Read Romans 14:17-19; Ephesians 6:15; Matthew 10:11-15

a. What is one of the things the Lord is revealing to us in this passage? Why? _____

_____

_____

_____

_____.

b. In Matthew 10:11-15, why did Jesus tell the disciples that if they found a suitable house in which to stay in each city where they went to preach and heal, but they were not accepted, they were to leave, shaking the very dust of that place off their feet? _____

_____

_____

_____.

c. Why does strife hinder our work? _____

_____

_____

_____

_____.

d. The Lord maintained inner peace and stability during the time He was on earth, regardless of His outward circumstances. If we want to do anything for our Lord and Savior, we need to_____

_____.

Why? _____

_____.

e. If we have a peaceful spirit, we will have a peaceful _____

_____.

7. Read 1 Timothy 1:8 MESSAGE

Why are gestures, voice tone, and facial expressions important?

_____

_____.

8. Read James 1:20,21; John 2:13-17

    a. In this passage, what does James tell us about man's anger?

    _____

    _____.

    b. Is there such a thing as righteous anger? _____

    _____

    _____.

    c. Did Jesus ever become angry? If so, give an example._____

    _____

    _____

    _____

    _____

    _____.

    d. Jesus' anger was not the wrong kind of anger; it was a right-
        eous anger, and we have the same right to display the same
        kind of anger that He did. That's why it is wrong to preach
        that we are never to get angry. However, the emotion of anger
        should submit to the spiritual fruit of self-control. How can
        the difference between the two kinds of anger be decided?

    _____

    _____

    _____.

9. Read Proverbs 31:26; review Matthew 12:34

    a. When we determine that nobody is ever going to hurt us
        again, what does that attitude influence? _____

    _____

    _____.

b. No matter how right your heart may be before the Lord, if you have _____ or _____ or _____ in your spirit, you cannot open your mouth without _____ _____ because Jesus told us, it is out of _____ _____ _____.

10. Read Matthew 11:29,30; review James 3:8

   a. Where is our main problem?_____ _____.

   b. As we have seen in this passage in James, who can tame the tongue?_____.

   c. There is something we can do about the tongue, and it is part of what Jesus was talking about when He told us to take His yoke upon us in Matthew 11:29,30. What is that? _____ _____ _____ _____ _____.

11. Read James 3:17

   a. How does this verse describe God's wisdom?_____ _____ _____ _____

_____
_____
_____
_____
_____
_____
_____.

b. It is wisdom to know when the time is to be _____ and _____, and when to be _____ and _____, to _____ _____, and to _____ _____.

12. Read James 3:18

a. Why does Satan try so hard to get you and me upset before we go to church and get the preacher upset before he steps up behind the pulpit? _____
_____
_____
_____
_____.

b. In light of this Scripture, we should not try to sow peace in the lives of others if we do not _____
_____.

c. In order for the Word of the Lord to take root, it must be sown _____

by someone who is _____.

d. That's why, if you intend or plan to work for the Lord, you must _____.

13. Read Joshua 24:15 KJV

a. Can the devil force us to get upset? If not, why do we do so?

_____

_____

_____.

b. How can we overcome past hurts and wounds that may cause us to react negatively? _____

_____

_____.

c. Since God has created us with a free will, with the ability to make our own decisions in life, what is the word He is sharing with us in our time? _____

_____

_____

_____

_____.

Speak No Evil

1. Review Proverbs 15:4; Ephesians 4:29

   a. In these passages and others throughout the Word of God, we are told to be careful how _____

   _____.

   b. We have already discussed Ephesians 4:29 about the words we speak, but it is such an important verse for this message that it is worth reviewing. What did Paul tell us to do in this passage? Why? _____

   _____

   _____

   _____

   _____

   _____

   _____

   _____

   _____

   _____.

   c. According to the writer of Proverbs, what does willful contrariness do? _____

   _____.

   d. What problem is created and magnified by wrong thoughts and words — our own or those of others? _____

   _____.

   e. We are not to use our mouths to _____, _____
   _____, or _____, but rather to
   _____, _____, and _____.

2. Review Romans 12:21

   a. Because we are children of light, in addition to magnifying
   Him, the Lord wants us to learn how to magnify the good in
   _____, in _____, and in
   _____.

   b. In this sense, "to magnify" means_____
   _____.

   c. When we magnify the Lord, what are we doing?_____
   _____
   _____.

   d. What does God want us to do with the good in our lives? ____
   _____
   _____.

3. Review 2 Corinthians 10:4

   a. What happens if the strongholds that are built up within
   us — especially in our minds — are not destroyed? _____
   _____
   _____.

   b. How is a stronghold like a brick wall? _____
   _____
   _____
   _____.

4. Read Numbers 13:32; review Matthew 12:36

    a. What truth in Numbers 13:32 should we lay hold on?_____
        _____.

    b. Not only are we not to talk negatively about our circum-
        stances, we are also not to talk negatively about _____
        _____.

    c. Most people have some good and some bad in them, just as
        we do. God doesn't want us to magnify the bad in others or
        in ourselves. He wants us to _____
        _____.

    d. When someone is acting badly toward us, what is the only
        thing that is going to make our situation better?_____
        _____
        _____.

    e. Why do we need to stop running to others, complaining
        about our situation? _____
        _____
        _____.

    f. It is not true that we should never talk about our problems;
        we just need to _____.

    g. In Matthew 12:36, what did Jesus say about our mouth? ___
        _____
        _____
        _____
        _____.

5. Read Numbers 13:25-28,30-33

    a. According to these passages, when the twelve Hebrew spies came back from their scouting expedition into the land of promise, only Joshua and Caleb gave a _____ report. The other ten gave an _____ report.

    b. Why is it that four out of five people can be defeated by a trial, while one can come through it victoriously? What is the difference? _____

        _____

        _____

        _____.

    c. Like the giants in the land of Canaan, whatever is magnified becomes_____

        _____.

    d. What is going to become most real to us? _____

        _____

        _____.

6. Read 2 Timothy 2:20,21; review Ephesians 4:29

    a. In light of 2 Timothy 2:20,21, how can we keep ourselves "fit and ready for any good work"? _____

        _____

        _____

        _____.

b. What two responsibilities do you and I have in regard to "evil reports"? _____

_____.

c. Each of us has a responsibility not _____

_____and not

_____.

d. As we have already seen, what has the Apostle Paul said in Ephesians 4:29? _____

_____

_____.

e. According to what Paul wrote to his young disciple Timothy, you and I are supposed to be clean vessels. We are to keep ourselves pure, and to help others to keep themselves pure as well. What is one way we do this? _____

_____

_____.

f. Why should we always be aware of our thoughts and words?

_____

_____.

7. Read Malachi 3:16

a. You and I have an opportunity to make glad the heart of God. In light of this Scripture, what is one way we do that?_____

_____

_____.

    b. There are proper ways to handle sensitive issues. The Bible says that God is listening to see _____ _____ _____.

8.   Read Numbers 13:29

    a. Each of the "ites" in this Scripture represented a different problem to the children of Israel. How did the evil report of the ten spies affect the millions of Israelites who were waiting for a decision about whether they should go cross over Jordan and take possession of their inheritance? _____ _____ _____.

    b. What opportunity do you and I have every day?_____ _____ _____ _____.

    c. Why has the Lord given us this message from His Word?_____ _____ _____.

9.   Read Ecclesiastes 3:1,7

    a. It is wisdom to be able to know _____ _____.

        But as a general rule, it is always timely to _____ _____.

b. Our fallen nature wants to_____

_____.

But our born-again nature wants to _____

_____.

10. Read Philippians 3:13,14; 1:6

a. The devil wants us to concentrate on our past and on our weaknesses, our losses, our problems. The Spirit of God wants us to focus on our strengths, our victories, our joys. In light of these passages of Scripture, what things should we be magnifying?_____

_____.

b. What things are always our ministry? _____

_____

_____.

c. What is always our calling?_____

_____

_____

_____

_____.

d. How do we magnify (make large) the good? _____

_____

_____

_____

_____.

e. If you are negative, what should you do? _____

_____

_____

_____

_____

_____

_____

_____

_____

_____

_____.

11. Read Malachi 2:5-7; Revelation 1:6

a. This Scripture in Malachi chapter 2 deals with priests and the kind of mouth that they are supposed to have. But according to Revelation 1:6, all of us are _____ and _____ because Jesus has ". . . formed us into a kingdom (a royal race), _____ to His God and Father. . . ."

b. In our covenant with the Lord, what is His part? _____

_____.

c. What is our part? _____

_____

_____.

d. If we have reverential and worshipful fear of the Lord, if we revere Him and stand in awe of His name, then we are not going to _____

_____

_____.

12. Read Romans 2:1; Matthew 7:1,2; 7:3-5 TLB

   a. What is the root of gossip, slander, backbiting, and talebearing? _____.

   b. What is the root of judgment? _____.

   c. Why do we speak evil of other people? _____

   _____

   _____.

   d. In light of the passages in Matthew chapter 7, why should you be very careful about criticizing and judging and condemning other people — especially believers? _____

   _____

   _____.

13. Read Malachi 2:6,7

   a. Since you and I are priests and kings to our God, what do we need to keep in our mouths?_____

   _____.

   b. What does that mean? _____

   _____

   _____.

14. Read 1 Peter 4:15; 1 Thessalonians 4:11; review Malachi 2:7

   a. One version of Webster's dictionary defines a "busybody" as

   _____

   _____.

   Another version of Webster's dictionary defines "busybody"

   as _____

   _____.

   The author defines "busybody" as _____

   _____

   _____.

   b. Webster's dictionary defines "gossip" as _____

   _____

   _____.

   The author defines "gossip" as _____

   _____

   _____.

   c. According to Vine, what are "slanderers"? _____

   _____

   _____

   _____.

   d. How does Webster's define "slander"? _____

   _____

   _____

   _____.

e. How is "whisper" defined in Webster's dictionary? What does a "whisperer" do? _____

_____

_____

_____

_____

_____

_____.

f. How does the Apostle Peter link all these together?

_____

_____.

g. What scriptural instruction do we find in 1 Thessalonians 4:11? _____

_____

_____.

h. How does God view exaggeration? _____.

i. Why does the Lord say that the lips of His priests are to guard and keep pure the knowledge of His law? _____

_____

_____

_____.

j. As God's messengers, His mouthpiece, you and I need to make sure that both _____ and _____ are in our mouths and that we _____

_____.

Chapter

13

A Soothing Tongue

1. Read Proverbs 8:6-9

   a. This passage should be not only our confession and testimony, but also our _____. That is, it should be not only what we say about ourselves, but also what _____.

   b. Unfortunately, all of us have learned in this life to speak in circles. We need to learn how to engage in _____ _____.

   c. As children of God, filled with His Spirit, what are we to manifest as our disposition?_____ _____ _____.

2. Read Proverbs 28:15 KJV

   a. How does Webster's define the word "disposition"? _____ _____ _____ _____ _____.

   b. What kind of disposition do you have? Are you a "grumpy bear" or are you a "teddy bear"? _____ _____ _____.

3. Read Proverbs 16:5

    a. What does this passage say about the Lord's view of everyone
        who has a proud disposition? What will be their fate? _____

        _____

        _____

        _____

        _____.

    b. Why are people with a proud disposition hard to deal with?

        _____

        _____.

    c. What are the characteristics of proud people? _____

        _____

        _____

        _____

        _____

        _____

        _____

        _____

        _____.

    d. Besides being on the defensive, proud people are also _____

        _____

        _____

        _____

        _____

        _____

_____

_____

_____

_____.

e. Proud people are usually not very happy people. How does this affect others? _____

_____.

4. Read Matthew 12:18-21

   a. As believers, as God's beloved children created in His image, what kind of disposition does He want us to have? _____

   _____

   _____.

   b. What kind of tongue does God want us to have in our mouths?_____

   _____

   _____.

   c. As God's messengers, His mouthpiece, His ambassadors of peace, how are we to be? _____

   _____

   _____.

   d. To do that, to be the way God wants us to be as His representatives on this earth, what are we going to have to do?

   _____

   _____

   _____.

5. Read Ephesians 4:22-24; 4:22 KJV; Proverbs 15:1 KJV

    a. Our nature is seen through our _____.
        That is to say that the kind of person we are is revealed by our

        _____.

    b. Our nature comes out of our _____.

    c. Proverbs 15:1 KJV is true for us — if we are willing to _____

        _____

        _____

        _____.

6. Read Matthew 11:28-30; Colossians 3:15; Hebrews 2:16 KJV

    a. Each of us has a different nature. No two of us are exactly
        alike. Our nature also changes as we go through the various
        experiences and cycles of life. Real change just doesn't come

        _____ or

        _____.

    b. There are no _____ saints or

        _____ ministries.

    c. If you and I are to be different from the way we are now, then
        we are going to have to _____

        _____. We are going

        to have to _____

        _____

        _____

        _____

        _____.

d. In Matthew 11:29, how does Jesus describe His nature?_____

_____

_____.

e. What does He say will happen if we will take His yoke — His nature — upon us and learn of Him? _____

_____.

f. In verse 30 how does Jesus describe His yoke — His nature?

_____

_____.

g. The Bible says that if we want to be led by the Spirit of God, we must learn to be led by _____.

h. If we are led by peace, then we can be assured that we are being led by God, because He is _____

_____.

i. If we are ever going to be truly happy, we are going to have to

_____

_____

_____.

j. What determines whether we are true worshippers of God?

_____

_____

_____.

7. Read Exodus 30:22-25; 2 Corinthians 2:15

    According to the Bible, there is a spiritual aroma that goes up from our lives when we are anointed with the Holy Ghost. What is it? _____

    _____.

8. Read Exodus 30:26-30

    a. According to Hannah Hurnard, the author of *Mountains of Spices*,[2] what does myrrh represent? Cinnamon? Calamus? ___

        _____

        _____.

    b. If you and I want the anointing of God upon us, then we are going to have to be imbued with_____

        _____

        _____.

9. Read Galatians 4:1,2; Romans 8:17 KJV; review Isaiah 58:6-9

    a. Why are we going to have to grow up and become mature in Christ?_____

        _____

        _____.

    b. When do we receive God's blessings? _____

        _____.

    c. What is one way we show we are mature? _____

        _____

        _____.

d. What is the Lord telling us in the passage in Isaiah 58:6-9?

_____

_____

_____

_____

_____.

10. Read 2 Peter 1:4-8; John 4:23; Philippians 2:13;
2 Timothy 4:7 KJV

a. In the passage in 2 Peter 1:4-8 is the biblical formula for mov-
ing out of the flesh and into the divine nature in order to
experience true Kingdom living. What are the three stages we
go through as we develop our relationship with God? _____

_____

_____

_____

_____.

b. We begin our Christian lives as newborn infants. We pray,
read the Bible, go to church, and worship _____,
or in the outer court. God accepts that kind of worship,
because He _____.

c. When God says to us, "It is time to move into the inner
court," part of that word comes through messages on holiness
which tell us that _____

_____.

d. Finally, God tells us that it's time to move into the Holy of Holies. In order to come into that place, our whole lives must be _____

_____

_____

_____

_____

_____

_____

_____

_____

_____.

e. In 2 Peter 1:4-8, what is the first thing we are told? _____

_____

_____.

f. Then what are we told to add to our diligence? _____

_____

_____.

g. What does excellence develop? _____

_____.

h. What does knowledge produce? _____

_____.

i. What does self-control lead to? _____.

j. What is steadfastness? _____

_____.

k. What is patience? _____

_____

_____.

l. What is happening as we are waiting? _____

_____

_____.

m. What do our steadfastness, patience, and endurance develop into?_____

_____.

n. What comes after godliness? What does it produce? _____

_____

_____.

11. Read 1 Peter 5:5; review 2 Peter 1:4-9

a. With what does Peter tell us to clothe (apron) ourselves?_____

_____

_____.

b. In light of the passage in 1 Peter 5:5, we in the body of Christ are to take on the cloak of _____

_____.

We are to wear that cloak _____

_____

_____

_____.

c. What comes after kindness?_____.

12. Read 2 Corinthians 3:18

    a. How does the change come that needs to take place in each
       of us? _____
       _____
       _____.

    b. What is the only thing that changes the inner man?_____
       _____
       _____
       _____.

    c. What kind of people is the Lord looking for? _____
       _____
       _____
       _____.

    d. What will happen if we are willing to be changed?_____
       _____
       _____
       _____
       _____.

    e. From what does fruit-bearing come? Explain. _____
       _____
       _____
       _____
       _____
       _____.

f. What should you do if you want to change, if you want to be like Jesus? _____

_____

_____.

Conclusion

1. In this study, what has the author tried to emphasize? _____
   _____
   _____
   _____.

2. What are *words*?_____.

3. Avoid all _____, _____,
   _____, and _____
   talk. Instead, learn to speak as _____ speaks.

4. What will the Word of God, spoken in truth and love from your
   lips, do?_____
   _____.

5. Why must your heart be right before the Lord in order to speak
   that Word in truth and love? _____
   _____
   _____
   _____
   _____.

6. You are bound by your _____, by your _____.
   You are also _____ by them.

7. Why is it so important to place a guard upon your lips? _____
   _____
   _____
   _____.

8. You can change your action and behavior, but to do so what must you first change? _____
_____.

9. What do you need to do that?_____
_____.

10. _____ determines action.

11. If you truly want your life to be totally different, what must you do?_____
_____
_____
_____.

Prayer for a
Personal Relationship
with the Lord

God wants you to receive His free gift of salvation. Jesus wants to save you and fill you with the Holy Spirit more than anything. If you have never invited Jesus, the Prince of Peace, to be your Lord and Savior, I invite you to do so now. Pray the following prayer, and if you are really sincere about it, you will experience a new life in Christ.

Father,

You loved the world so much, You gave Your only begotten Son to die for our sins so that whoever believes in Him will not perish, but have eternal life.

Your Word says we are saved by grace through faith as a gift from You. There is nothing we can do to earn salvation.

I believe and confess with my mouth that Jesus Christ is Your Son, the Savior of the world. I believe He died on the cross for me and bore all of my sins, paying the price for them. I believe in my heart that You raised Jesus from the dead.

I ask You to forgive my sins. I confess Jesus as my Lord. According to Your Word, I am saved and will spend eternity with You! Thank You, Father. I am so grateful! In Jesus' name, amen.

See John 3:16; Ephesians 2:8,9; Romans 10:9,10; 1 Corinthians 15:3,4; 1 John 1:9; 4:14-16; 5:1,12,13.

Answers

Introduction

1. The mind or intellect, the will, and the emotions.
2. Because it is full of "self."
3a. To what we think, feel, and want.
3b. What we think, not necessarily what God thinks.
3c. What we want, not what God wants.
3d. What we feel, not what God feels.
4. It is trained to carry God's thoughts, desires, and feelings; then we become a mouthpiece for the Lord!
5. That we have been given the mind of Christ and that we hold the thoughts, feelings, and purposes of His heart.
6. The body and soul corporately.
7. Come under the leadership of the Spirit; requires time and diligence.
8. Either to the flesh or to the spirit. It can be used to verbalize God's Word or as a vehicle to express the enemy's work.
9. "Death"; "life"; "eat the fruit of it [for death or life]."
10. It can be used to bring blessings or destruction not only to our own lives, but also to the lives of many others.

Chapter 1

1a. Talk *to* them.
1b. Not our will, but the will of God. His will is His Word.
1c. With the Word of God. He repeatedly said, "It is written," and quoted Scriptures that met the lies and deceptions of the devil head on.
1d. We stop speaking the Word to our problems and begin once again speaking our feelings, which is probably what got us into trouble to begin with.
1e. Know what we believe and be determined to stick with it until we see results.
2a. He will be sadly disappointed.
2b. Unforgiveness.
2c. Trying to operate one of God's principles while completely ignoring another.
2d. Obedience.
2e. Repentance and a return to submission and obedience.

3a. The "ifs" and "buts."

3b. By honoring Him with obedience in our relationships.

3c. Opens the door for the blessing that is already there due to God's goodness to flow to us.

4. How to talk God's way.

5a. Know His heart and be led by His Spirit.

5b. Time.

6a. Salvation.

6b. We ask with wrong purpose and evil, selfish motives.

6c. "If it be Thy will."

6d. The spiritual life becomes a tragedy instead of a triumph.

6e. Let God be God.

7a. Extremes.

7b. To get him so one-sided and out of balance with that truth that he is no better off than he was before.

7c. Wisdom.

7d. "1. Understanding what is true, right, or lasting. 2. Good judgment: common sense."[1]

7e. Prudence; prudence is good management.

7f. "Using good judgment or common sense in handling practical matters."[2]

7g. A combination of balance, common sense, and good judgment.

7h. Is in line with God's Word and will for you at this particular time in your life.

7i. You will see the will of God accomplished in your life.

Chapter 2

1a. His salvation before men, but not before God, and his position before the enemy of his soul.

1b. A change in allegiance. Previously he has served the devil, but notice is now being given that he is changing masters.

1c. As "to make firm, establish, make secure"[1] and "to make valid, ratify, impart authority or influence."[2]

1d. "Of authoritative validity."[3]

1e. It "nails salvation in place."

2a. The written Word of God.

2b.   His faith-filled words go forth to establish God's order in his life.

2c.   Things begin to change!

3a.   Has been established in the spiritual realm since before the foundation of the earth.

3b.   ". . . thoughts and plans for welfare and peace and not for evil. . . ." To give us hope in our final outcome.

3c.   It literally begins to become reality.

3d.   Bring their mouths as well as their hearts into God's service.

3e.   Talking like the devil.

3f.   We will not see positive results in our daily lives.

3g.   Calling for. We are reaching into the realm of the spirit and drawing out according to our words.

3h.   Evil, negative things.

3i.   Good, positive things.

4a.   God's mighty words.

4b.   We are created in God's image (Genesis 1:26,27), and we are supposed to act like Him.

5.   By speaking of those things that He has promised in His Word to us as if they already existed.

6a.   Win them to Christ.

6b.   Spiritual knowledge and understanding.

6c.   The fruit of love, the "more excellent way"; is not rude or unmannerly.

6d.   By love.

6e.   Fact.

6f.   We can "declare the decree" in private; then when someone asks how we are doing or how we are feeling, we can find a way to remain positive and yet not leave the other person thinking that Christians (along with everything they believe) are weird.

6g.   "Spiritually."

6h.   Wisdom; common sense. The Holy Spirit.

Chapter 3

1a.   That of reaching into the realm where God is and calling "those things which be not as if they were" (author's paraphrase).

1b.   Speaking forth the words that will shape their future.

2a.   "Declaring the decree!"

2b.   Yes, as long as we are reasonably sure that what we are declaring is God's will for our life and not just what we want.

2c.   Muttering,[1] conversing aloud with oneself, or declaring something.[2]

2d.   It helps establish it in the heart.

3a.   They needed a new self-image before their miracle could occur.

3b.   The future was being prophesied: Abraham would be the father of a multitude, and Sarah would be the mother of nations.

3c.   Reaching into the realm of the spirit, where their miracle was.

3d.   Draw out the miracle God had promised. Coming into agreement with God's Word, as spoken earlier in Genesis 15.

4a.   Abram believed God.

4b.   We believe that God can do the impossible and that He will do it for us.

4c.   To release their faith.

4d.   It helps keep our faith strong until our manifestation arrives.

4e.   We are willing to agree with Him — in our hearts and with our words.

5a.   To mentally agree with God or believe what He tells us.

5b.   Because what is in our hearts will come out of our mouths.

5c.   To what is in our souls.

5d.   Whatever our souls are full of.

5e.   We will draw those things to ourselves.

5f.   That is what we will draw to us.

5g.   The choice is ours!

Chapter 4

1a.   ". . . if anyone does not offend in speech [never says the wrong things]. . . ."

1b.   Words are very important and powerful, and we will be held responsible for them: "For by your words you will be justified and acquitted, and by your words you will be condemned and sentenced."

2a.   Not by himself.

2b.   It is wild and uncontrollable, always wanting to do its own thing.

2c.   The help of the Holy Spirit.

2d.   Learn to discipline our own mouths and take responsibility for what comes out of them.

2e. Cooperating with God, taking His Word and starting to speak it over your life.

2f. Yes. By speaking evil of it. Yes. By speaking well of it.

2g. A lie.

2h. "Liar . . . and the father of lies and of all that is false."

2i. He strives to give us trouble and then use it to influence us to prophesy that same kind of trouble in our future.

3a. 1) No person's words have as much authority in our life as our own, and 2) our future cannot be blessed until we let go of the past.

3b. By no longer considering (thinking about) the things of old, believing that God has a good plan for our future.

3c. Begin to think in agreement with God. Begin to speak in agreement with Him. Actually prophesy our own future.

4a. Because words are containers for power; they carry creative or destructive power.

4b. That in the tongue is the power of life and death.

4c. Carry weight in the spiritual realm.

5a. To *yourself*.

5b. Faith-filled words, believing, as Jesus said, that the words you speak are spirit and life. Speak life into your life, not death.

6a. Watch for the attacks of the enemy and pray immediately.

6b. He will never get a stronghold!

7a. Positives; negatives.

7b. The Word of God.

7c. In the spiritual realm.

7d. Defeats a spiritual (unseen) enemy.

8a. We will win.

8b. Declaring in the beginning what will happen in the end.

9a. First, He declares things; then He does them.

9b. Spiritual laws; cannot ignore them.

9c. Words are seeds. We sow word seeds and reap according to what we have sown.

10a. Speak forth and declare the Word of the Lord — *before it comes to pass*.

10b. By prophesying (speaking forth God's Word) over your own life at any time.

11a. Stop speaking the old things and start speaking some new things.

11b.   By finding out what God's Word promises you and beginning to declare the end from the beginning.

11c.   By saying about your situation what you believe He would say, you will open the door for the miracle-working power of God.

Chapter 5

1a.   Mouthpiece.

1b.   Their mouth and what comes out of it.

2a.   Speak only when spoken through.

2b.   Our mouth must belong to Him.

3a.   "The way" by their lives as well as by the Word of God.

3b.   The mouth.

3c.   Encouragement, comfort; edification.

4a.   That he ". . . should know how to speak a word in season to him who is weary. . . ."

4b.   The words of our mouth; speak life to them.

4c.   "A word in season," a word that will heal and encourage them.

5a.   ". . . encourage (admonish, exhort) one another and edify (strengthen and build up) one another. . . ."

5b.   The "gift of exhortation." One of the ministry gifts that the Holy Spirit confers upon certain individuals.

5c.   "Helper." Exhorts people in their growth in God, encouraging them to be all they can be, for God's glory. As a Helper and an Exhorter, He anoints others for that ministry.

5d.   A ministry; a much needed ministry.

5e.   Backsliding or giving up!

5f.   Exhorters bring comfort; they just simply make people feel better — about themselves, about their circumstances, about the past, about the present, about the future, about anything else that concerns them.

5g.   To continue in exhorting one another.

5h.   People are hurting and need to be encouraged.

6a.   ". . . only such [speech] as is good and beneficial to the spiritual progress of others, as is fitting to the need and the occasion, that it may be a blessing and give grace (God's favor) to those who hear it."

6b.   By the grace gift that was upon him. (Romans 12:3.)

6c.   Out of balance.

6d.   Mouths; mouthpiece.

6e.   Without God's cleansing power we are all people of unclean lips. (Isaiah 6:5.)

Chapter 6

1a.   Complaining is a sin! It is a corrupt form of conversation that causes many people a great deal of problems in their lives.

1b.   It opens many doors for the enemy.

1c.   Power.

1d.   They destroy the joy of the one doing the complaining and can also affect other people who have to listen to them.

1e.   Murmuring and complaining probably sound like cursing to Him. It is verbal pollution.

1f.   When we complain about our current situation we remain in it, when we praise God in the midst of difficulty, He raises us out of it.

1g.   Gratitude; thanksgiving.

1h.   They are too busy being grateful for the good things they do have; they have no time to notice the things they could complain about.

1i.   Good; evil. Good; evil. (See Romans 12:21.)

1j.   Overcome it with good.

1k.   Good; evil.

2a.   They can bring healing or they can open the door for disease.

2b.   Healing power.

2c.   It can actually destroy it.

2d.   Physical energy; healing.

3a.   He takes it personally. He considers that we are exploiting His goodness. God is good, and He wants to hear us tell Him and others about His goodness.

3b.   Giving a critical appraisal of the God we serve.

3c.   For our instruction, so we can see their mistakes and not make the same ones. We should heed their example and not follow their pattern.

4a.   Guards his words can keep himself from ruin; does not guard his words can bring destruction into his own life.

4b.   The Israelites complained and after four decades they were still wandering in the wilderness of death and destruction. Jesus continued to praise God no matter what, refusing to complain, and as a result God raised Him from death to new life.

4c.   We should guard against the temptation to complain and grumble, and instead purposely *choose* to offer up the sacrifice of praise and thanksgiving. (Hebrews 13:15 KJV.)

4d.   Complain and remain; praise and be raised.

5a.   Thanksgiving.

5b.   Weakens; releases power — power to bring answers to our prayers.

5c.   Spiritually mature enough to handle any type of promotion or increase.

5d.   If we don't feel like it, or if our circumstances don't dictate it, thanksgiving can become a sacrificial offering, made by faith, in obedience, because we love the Lord and want to honor His Word.

6a.   Only after he had offered the sacrifice of thanksgiving.

6b.   Negative (evil) power.

7a.   Constantly and at all times.

7b.   Things to complain about; reasons to give God glory.

7c.   "At all times"; "in every circumstance"; "for everything."

7d.   *For; in.*

7e.   Powerful.

8a.   The mouth.

8b.   Negative talk, complaining, grumbling, and all the related types of speech.

9a.   "Voice your thankfulness to God."

9b.   Complaining; critical; faultfinding.

9c.   Excuses of any kind.

9d.   Excuses; choke fruit.

9e.   Addicted.

9f.   Whistling for the devil. The devil, who will quickly come in to give us more misery.

9g.   Pride.

9h.   By humbling ourselves and realizing how blessed we are to have anything at all.

9i.   Major on the positive attributes and minor on the negative ones.

10a.   Unthankful; ungrateful.

10b.   Express gratitude to God.

11a.   The spirit of the world today.

11b. Living epistles, read of all men.

11c. By a lifestyle that lifts up His principles.

11d. So that we may be able to show the world a different way of living.

12a. Complain; find fault. It simply means that we make it our goal in life to be as positive as possible.

12b. The fruit of the lips will change.

12c. Sweeten your relationship with the Lord.

13. Provide us with negative circumstances.

14a. Complain; in the beginning.

14b. Sow seeds now for our future.

14c. More of what we are grumbling about. A bountiful harvest later on.

15a. A pledge of what was to come.

15b. A beginning of a great downpour. A pledge or foretaste of good things to come.

16a. It is a sign of greater things to come.

16b. By complaining over it.

16c. By believing over it.

16d. We will never see the harvest.

16e. "Be content with what you have."

16f. By faith. We know that the Lord is the Author and the Finisher. (Hebrews 12:2.) What He begins, He completes. (Philippians 1:6.) He will do that for us — *if* we will hold our faith firm until the end. (Hebrews 3:6.)

Chapter 7

1a. During a storm.

1b. Behave in the storm!

1c. He "decided" that it would be wise not to open His mouth. In His humanity He would have been tempted to do the same thing you and I do: doubt, question God, complain, say something negative, etc.

1d. Be quieter than usual.

1e. Be quiet and allow the emotional storm to subside.

2. It is time for a change.

3a. The middle where we encounter the storms.

3b. Place of testing.

3c. "The midnight hour"; "the dark night of the soul."

3d.   "Use" our faith.

3e.   Just how much faith we really have.

3f.   "Using" it; talking about it.

3g.   Equips us to handle the next one better.

3h.   Know that we will win before the battle ever starts.

3i.   Manifestation. Middle.

4a.   Calmed; rebuked.

4b.   Grow in faith, which is confidence and trust in God.

4c.   Grow in self-control and discipline of the mouth.

5a.   Hold fast our confession of faith; God has His eye on everything, including us and the storm.

5b.   He will not allow us to sink.

6a.   Saying one thing in good times and another in hard times.

6b.   Control. Maturity. Glorify.

7a.   "Worthless (futile, barren)."

7b.   "A harness consisting of a headstall, bit, and reins, which fits a horse's head and is used to restrain or guide."[1]

7c.   We may never experience deliverance.

7d.   The Holy Spirit, if we accept His leadership and guidance.

8a.   Our tongue gives direction to all the rest of our life. Our words draw borders for us, and we must live inside those borders.

8b.   As, "The metal mouthpiece of a bridle that controls and curbs an animal. . . . Something that controls. . . ."[2]

8c.   When we begin to say the wrong thing, we will sense Him trying to pull us in the right direction.

9a.   Bit and bridle. We will end up at the right place and stay out of all the wrong places.

9b.   We will end up with a lot of pain.

10a. Our thoughts.

10b. We are to lead every wrong thought captive unto the obedience of Jesus Christ. Second Corinthians 10:5 KJV tells us to cast down wrong imaginations.

10c. It must be renewed completely. (Romans 12:1,2.)

10d. It is our choice.

10e. "... whatever is true, whatever is worthy of reverence and is honorable and seemly, whatever is just, whatever is pure, whatever is lovely and lovable, whatever is kind and winsome and gracious . . . ."

10f. Because they work together.

11a. God's will.

11b. Through the eye of faith.

11c. They have never learned how to talk.

11d. Times of personal difficulty.

11e. Turn around and go back to where you came from.

11f. "... they endure for a little while; then when trouble or persecution arises on account of the Word, they immediately are offended (become displeased, indignant, resentful) and they stumble and fall away."

11g. He has overcome the world.

12a. We become His mouthpiece and prophesy His Word.

12b. Our own idle words; our mouths to take the lead role.

13a. Dead circumstance.

13b. God will make a way.

14a. She kept *saying!*

14b. Through her words.

14c. Through our words.

14d. Keep saying — and don't give up hope!

15a. We must be filled with hope, we must think hope, and we must talk hope. Hope is the foundation on which faith stands.

15b. Restore to us double everything we have lost.

16a. Because anything that offends God in our conversation needs to be eliminated.

16b. Purpose to keep our mouth from transgressing.

16c. Because nothing gets God's attention any quicker. It is His Word that carries the power of the Holy Spirit.

16d. You will begin to notice that you are changing.

16e. God-ordained results.

Chapter 8

1a. Mouth.

1b. "Working out."

1c.   Deposits a seed in us, and then we must cooperate with the work of the Holy Spirit to see that the seed He has placed in us grows into a plant that occupies our entire life.

2a.   As "the seed."

2b.   Harvest.

2c.   Everything good that God desires for us to have.

2d.   God. It must be cultivated, nurtured, watered, and cared for.

2e.   It must be kept plowed up and weed free.

2f.   Our hearts and lives.

2g.   By submitting to the Holy Spirit our wills, which means submitting the flesh to the leadership of the spirit.

2h.   We would be amazed at how different we are now from what we were when we began.

2i.   A life-changing revelation on *the mouth!*

3.   He had to do something about their words, about their mouths, before He could use them the way He had planned.

4a.   Because he immediately began to say things that God had *not* told him to say.

4b.   No.

4c.   What God says about us!

4d.   "I speak not My own words, but the words of the One Who sent Me. I say only what I have heard My Father say." (John 8:28; 12:50, author's paraphrase.)

4e.   Soul; spirit.

5a.   New opposition.

5b.   Open doors for the enemy that we don't want to open.

5c.   Walk in the flesh until it is time to exercise our ministry gift, and then quickly try to get in the Spirit.

5d.   There are things that must be moved out of the way in order for it to be ushered in.

5e.   Rejoice over what is coming!

6a.   That he wasn't eloquent enough to do what God wanted done because he had a "mouth problem."

6b.   He does.

6c.   "Now therefore go, and I will be with your mouth and will teach you what you shall say."

6d. Remember, if He has sent you, He will be with your mouth and will teach you what to say.

7a. He needs to cleanse our mouth.

7b. He is going to deal with us.

7c. Put us through a cleansing process.

7d. His heart was to serve the Lord, which God already knew before He drew him into His Presence.

7e. God will always look for someone who has a perfect heart toward Him, not necessarily someone who has a perfect performance before Him. When the Lord has the heart, He can always change the behavior.

7f. Molds and makes us into vessels fit for His use.

7g. Call; anointing; appointment; different time periods.

8a. Lay the proper foundation.

8b. Getting the mouth in line.

9a. Some things about their mouths.

9b. Realize that we need healing.

9c. "My mouth needs to be saved!"

Chapter 9

1. What He considers to be "true fasting."

2a. The purpose of breaking the power of the flesh. It is meant to be a time of special prayer in which God's people seek Him in a more serious manner for breakthrough for themselves or for others.

2b. No, there are many varieties of ways that people are led to fast.

3a. ". . . to loose the bonds of wickedness, to undo the bands of the yoke, to let the oppressed go free, and that you break every [enslaving] yoke."

3b. Sit around and allow ourselves to remain in bondage.

3c. Cooperate with the Spirit of God. If we are to be able to set others free, we must first be set free ourselves.

4a. ". . . to divide your bread with the hungry and bring the homeless poor into your house — when you see the naked, that you cover him, and that you hide not yourself from [the needs of] your own flesh and blood."

4b. Those around us in the world, the poor and the naked, and also our flesh and blood, our own family and relatives.

5. Our doing certain things.

6a. He has told us to take away from our midst the yokes of oppression, to stop pointing the finger in scorn toward the oppressed or the godly, and to stop speaking falsely, harshly, unjustly, and wickedly.

6b. We are not doing what God has plainly told us to do.

6c. Stop judging one another.

6d. Falsely, harshly, unjustly, wickedly.

6e. It is useless speech, nonsense talk.

6f. Talking too much.

6g. Exercise careful control over our words.

7a. When we stop judging each other and put away from ourselves every form of vain, false, harsh, unjust, and wicked speaking.

7b. Pour out of our mouths curses on others.

8a. "If you really want to enjoy My blessings in this life, then don't run around doing your own thing. Instead, find out what I want you to do — and then do it. Don't seek your own pleasure, but seek first My will. Don't speak your own idle words, but speak My powerful words, for they will not come back void, without producing any effect, useless."

8b. To bless God, to bless others, and to bless ourselves.

8c. Live godly lives before them.

8d. Bring forth a sweet-smelling aroma, pleasing to others and pleasing to God.

8e. By oozing with the fruit of the Spirit, with kindness, gentleness, goodness, love, joy, peace, and all the other fruit.

8f. God.

8g. "Let the words of my mouth and the meditation of my heart be acceptable in Your sight, O Lord, my [firm, impenetrable] Rock and my Redeemer."

Chapter 10

1a. It means that you and I go through life with an awesome power — like fire or electricity or nuclear energy — right under our noses, one that can produce death or life, depending on how it is used.

1b. Good; evil; benefit; harm.

1c. We can use it to create death and destruction, or we can use it to create life and health.

1d. We can speak forth sickness, disease, dissention, and disaster, or we can speak forth healing, harmony, exhortation, and edification.

1e. The choice is ours.

2a.   Whatever we sow is what we will reap.

2b.   Right under your nose.

2c.   The choice of our words.

2d.   If we are a blabbermouth, we are going to get into trouble.

2e.   We get unsettled and lose our peace — not necessarily because we are saying something evil, but simply because we need to be quiet and listen.

3a.   To keep one ear tuned to God.

3b.   To be quick to hear and slow to speak.

3c.   We might not say some of the things we say.

3d.   So that he would know how to "speak a word in season" to the weary.

3e.   The joy of the Lord.

3f.   In Christ alone.

3g.   Speaking words in due season to one another.

4a.   It disturbs Him that with the same mouth we use to bless and praise Him, we curse and condemn our fellow man, made in His image just as we are.

4b.   Realize that we have a long way to go before we become perfect.

4c.   The Lord looks upon our heart and counts us as perfect while we are on the way to becoming so.

4d.   Those who are guilty of finding fault with others and spreading criticism.[1]

4e.   No. Something can be spread if it is told to only one other person.

4f.   It means that when you and I slander someone or accuse another person falsely, we are allowing the devil to use our mouths.

4g.   Because He wants to do something good in our lives, but our mouths are affecting our anointing.

4h.   Somebody wounded or even broke their spirit so that they ended up with a failure image.

5a.   Healer of the brokenhearted.

5b.   He will heal you so you can go forth and bring that healing to someone else. Those whom you have hurt will also forgive you and receive healing.

5c.   Don't break another person's spirit!

6a.   How wives and husbands are to regard and treat one another in the Lord.

6b.   To "adapt" themselves to their husbands.

6c.   Calling in Christ Jesus.

6d.   To be affectionate and sympathetic to their wives. It means that they are to be considerate of them, not harsh or unkind or bitter toward them.

6e.   Just be sweet, kind, nice, and encouraging!

7a.   He has a strong spirit within him to sustain him in those times of trouble.

7b.   The encourager or exhorter.

7c.   Because every time we get around them, they make us feel better by the things they say and do. It just seems to come natural to them to uplift, encourage, and strengthen others by their very presence and personality.

7d.   We can encourage. We can exhort. We can build up, edify, lift up, and speak life. We can refuse to be slanderers. We can refuse to do the work of the devil with the words of our mouth.

8a.   Take our burden to the Lord; He will hear us and help us.

8b.   Pray; sow.

8c.   Start being an exhorter!

8d.   The healing balm of Gilead begins to drip down into that person's wounded soul. Suddenly he begins to think, "Yes, I believe I can make it!"

8e.   Comfort us; encourage us; urge us to press on; propel us forward.

8f.   Slander, accuse, find fault, and spread innuendoes and criticism; encourage, strengthen, help, inspire, and comfort.

8g.   The devil; the Holy Spirit.

Chapter 11

1a.   Wrath, passion, rage, bad temper, resentment, anger, animosity, quarreling, brawling, clamor, contention, slander, evil-speaking, abusive or blasphemous language, malice, spite, ill will, or baseness of any kind.

1b.   (Your answer.)

1c.   No. We have the ability in the Holy Spirit to be adjustable and adaptable.

2a.   Quick; slow; slow; slow.

2b.   Being slow to speak.

2c.   Acceptance with joy.

2d.   It is not going to reverse your bad situation.

3a.   Adaptable; adjustable. Pliable; moldable.

3b.   Pride and self-concern or self-centeredness.

3c.   We are entitled to have everything our way.

4a.   Selfishness. Our flesh (that is, our carnal nature) just loves itself. It always wants its own way.

4b.   First, to prove they are right, because we all want to be right. And second, to have their way, because we all want to have our way in everything.

4c.   Calm down and exercise a bit more humility, realizing that the minor things we fuss and argue over don't make that much difference in life anyway.

4d.   Our willingness to dwell together in peace and harmony.

5a.   "Love endures long and is patient and kind; love never is envious nor boils over with jealousy, is not boastful or vainglorious, does not display itself haughtily. It is not conceited (arrogant and inflated with pride); it is not rude (unmannerly) and does not act unbecomingly. Love (God's love in us) does not insist on its own rights or its own way. . . ."

5b.   Love.

5c.   By dying to self on a daily basis.

5d.   Two reasons: because we want to be right, and because we want our way, which is selfishness.

5e.   Love, which is caring more for the opinions and desires of others than for our own.

5f.   To come up higher, to give up trying to have everything our own way all the time, and to remember that whatever is in your heart eventually comes out of your mouth. (Matthew 12:34.)

6a.   The vital necessity of walking in peace. According to Ephesians 6:15, peace is part of the armor of God with which we are to clothe ourselves.

6b.   If they remained in a house or city that was in strife, they could not do any real work there.

6c.   Because it grieves the Holy Spirit. When peace leaves, the Holy Spirit leaves, and He is the One Who does the real work.

6d.   Learn to hunger and thirst after peace. Because it is in this area that Satan is stealing from God's people.

6e.   Mouth.

7.   They all convey a message, just as much as words do.

8a.   It does not promote the righteousness of God.

8b.   Yes, there are times when it is all right to get mad and display anger.

8c.   Yes. He cleaned out the temple because the people were defiling the house of God by buying and selling in it and not genuinely caring for the people.

8d. By what is called in the Bible "the law of kindness."

9a. Our words and speech.

9b. Pride; anger; resentment; expressing those negative traits and emotions; the abundance of the heart or spirit that the mouth speaks.

10a. Right under our noses — in our mouths.

10b. No man.

10c. We can submit it to God, asking that His Spirit take command of our tongue and bring it into submission to His will and way.

11a. ". . . the wisdom from above is first of all pure (undefiled); then it is peace-loving, courteous (considerate, gentle). [It is willing to] yield to reason, full of compassion and good fruits; it is wholehearted and straight-forward, impartial and unfeigned (free from doubts, wavering, and insincerity)."

11b. Patient and forbearing; firm and decisive; "be not angry"; display righteous indignation.

12a. Because he does not want us to gather together in an attitude of peace. He knows that if we are in turmoil inside, the words we hear will bounce right off us. They will not take root.

12b. Get the strife out of our own life.

12c. In a ground of peace; walking in peace.

12d. Get the strife out of your life.

13a. No. Because we have chosen to do so. The choice is always ours.

13b. By learning the Word of God and choosing to act upon it rather than to *re*-act to circumstances.

13c. The same one He told the children of Israel in the days of Joshua: "Choose you this day." In other words, "Grow up!"

Chapter 12

1a. We use our mouths, to pay attention to our words.

1b. "Let no foul or polluting language, nor evil word nor unwholesome or worthless talk [ever] come out of your mouth, but only such [speech] as is good and beneficial to the spiritual progress of others, as is fitting to the need and the occasion, that it may be a blessing and give grace (God's favor) to those who hear it."

1c. It breaks down the spirit.

1d. Depression of the human spirit.

1e. Hurt; break down; depress; heal; restore; uplift.

2a. Life; others; ourselves.

2b. To make larger.

2c. Making God larger than all our problems.

2d. To make it larger than the bad.

3a. They are going to cause us trouble.

3b. It is built up one brick at a time by rotating certain kinds of thoughts in the mind.

4a. Evil reports God considers negative reports.

4b. Other people.

4c. Magnify the good.

4d. Turning our face toward the Lord and crying out to Him to help us.

4e. Because every time we do so we add another brick to the stronghold that is being built up in our lives.

4f. Speak with purpose.

4g. We are going to be held accountable for our vain, useless conversation, what the *King James Version* calls "every idle word."

5a. Favorable; evil or negative.

5b. Because of the way they look at it. The one chooses to magnify the good, while the others choose to magnify the bad.

5c. Bigger and bigger in the eyes of the one doing the magnifying.

5d. Whatever you and I talk about — whether negative or positive.

6a. By cleansing ourselves "from what is ignoble and unclean," separating ourselves "from contact with contaminating and corrupting influences."

6b. One is not to give them, and the second is not to receive them.

6c. To talk to the other negatively; to let the other talk to us that way.

6d. That we are not to be involved in polluting our own minds or the minds of those around us.

6e. By thinking and speaking the way that God wants us to think and speak.

6f. Because God hears them and records them in His book of remembrance.

7a. By magnifying Him in our conversation.

7b. How we handle ourselves in all the circumstances we encounter in this life.

8a. They picked up the same spirit that was within them, and they began to murmur and doubt and fear.

8b. The opportunity of giving the good report or the evil report, of magnifying the Lord or magnifying the enemy.

8c.   So we will choose to use our mouths not to speak evil, but to speak good.

9a.   When to speak and when not to. Exhort and encourage others.

9b.   Find fault with others and magnify problems. Bless others and to magnify the good.

10a. The works of the Lord and not the works of the devil.

10b. Exhortation, encouragement, and edification.

10c. To urge others to keep being all they can be in Christ Jesus and to encourage them to keep straining forward toward the prize.

10d. By talking about it, by being positive in our thoughts, in our attitudes, in our outlook, in our words, and in our actions.

10e. Surrender your will to the Lord, Who is all positive. Say to Him, "O Lord, I want to be like You. Help me to be positive and not to be negative anymore." Ask God to change you! Do whatever God tells you to do. Cooperate with His Spirit and follow His leadership and guidance as you move from darkness to light, from negativism to positivism, from death to life.

11a. Kings; priests; "priests."

11b. To give us life and peace.

11c. To give Him reverence and worshipful fear, to revere Him, and to stand in awe of His name.

11d. Use our mouths to speak evil against His people for whom we serve as His priests.

12a. Judgment.

12b. Pride.

12c. Because we think we are better than they are.

12d. Because it is a violation of your divine calling.

13a. The law of truth.

13b. Not judging or criticizing or condemning, not being a gossip or a busybody.

14a. "One who concerns himself with other people's affairs."[1] "A nosy, meddlesome person."[2] One who digs up evil reports and makes it his business to spread them by gossip, slander, whispering, and so forth.

14b. As "n. . . . one who habitually repeats intimate or private rumors or facts," "vi. . . . To engage in or spread gossip."[3] One who magnifies and sensationalizes rumors and partial information.

14c. "Those who are given to finding fault with the demeanor and conduct of others, and spreading their innuendos and criticisms in the church."[4]

14d. "*n.* . . . Utterance of defamatory statements injurious to the reputation or well-being of a person. A malicious report or statement," "*vt.* . . . To utter damaging reports about."[5]

14e. "*n.* . . . A surreptitiously or secretly expressed belief, rumor, or hint <a *whisper* of impropriety>," "*vt.* . . . To speak quietly or privately, as when imparting gossip, slander, or intrigue."[6] A *whisperer* speaks quietly or privately to surreptitiously or secretly impart gossip, slander, or intrigue.

14f. As being sin in the eyes of God.

14g. To mind our own business.

14h. As much a sin as any of these others.

14i. Because the people seek, inquire, and require instruction at the mouth of the priest, who is the messenger of God.

14j. The law of truth; the law of kindness; speak no evil with our lips.

Chapter 13

1a. Reputation. Others say about us.

1b. Plain, straightforward, honest, truthful communication.

1c. The fruits of the Spirit, especially kindness, gentleness, meekness, and humility.

2a. "One's usual mood: TEMPERAMENT," "habitual tendency or inclination," or "usual manner of emotional response."[1]

2b. (Your answers.)

3a. "Everyone proud and arrogant in heart is disgusting, hateful, and exceedingly offensive to the Lord; be assured [I pledge it] they will not go unpunished."

3b. Because they are so arrogant.

3c. They can't be told anything because they already know everything. Since they are so opinionated, they are always on the defensive, which makes it hard for them to receive correction because to them that would be an admission they are wrong — and that is something they find almost impossible to do.

3d. Usually busy trying to convince others how they need to change or what they need to do. Proud people feel that they have to convince others that they are right and others are wrong. Proud people are also usually very rigid, which explains why they are often such strict disciplinarians. Finally, proud people are often complicated people.

3e. They do not make very many other people happy either.

4a. The same soothing disposition that His Son Jesus displayed.

4b. One that brings encouragement and edification and exhortation everywhere we go.

4c. Soothing and kind, simple and humble, pliable and adaptable.

4d. Put off our old nature and put on the new nature — which is the nature of His beloved Son Jesus Christ.

5a. Conversation; speech.

5b. Mouth.

5c. Lay aside our pride and allow the Holy Spirit to work through us as He wills in every situation.

6a. Easily; quickly.

6b. Overnight; instant.

6c. Endure some suffering. Cooperate with the Lord as step by step He brings us into conformity to His will and way, gradually transforming us into the image of His Son Jesus.

6d. He says that He is gentle, meek, humble, and lowly of heart.

6e. We will find rest.

6f. As wholesome and good, not harsh, hard, sharp, or pressing, but comfortable, gracious, and pleasant.

6g. Peace.

6h. The peace that is on the inside of us.

6i. Be like Jesus, to take His nature upon us, even as He took our nature upon Himself.

6j. Whether we are harsh and hard or sweet and soothing.

7. "The sweet fragrance of Christ."

8a. Meekness.[3] Goodness.[4] Gentleness.[5]

8b. A mixture of meekness, goodness, gentleness, and humility.

9a. So that we may claim the full inheritance set apart for the children of God.

9b. Only when we are mature enough to handle them.

9c. By demonstrating that we have control of our mouths.

9d. That He wants us to have the same kind of mature disposition that His Son Jesus had, one that is not selfish and self-centered, but one that cares for others.

10a. We start our relationship with God in the outer court. From there we move into the inner court, and then finally into the Holy of Holies.[6]

10b. In the flesh. Takes us where we are.

10c. God used to allow certain things, but not anymore.

10d. Placed upon the altar before the Lord. We cannot reserve the little things that we want for ourselves. We must give it all up to God, becoming true worshippers in spirit and in truth. That means that we must be ready to live our lives before Him as He desires, trusting Him to give us the grace to do so.

10e. That we must take the promises of God and add to them diligence.

10f. Faith, which in turn develops virtue or excellence.

10g. Knowledge.

10h. Self-control.

10i. Steadfastness.

10j. Patience or endurance.

10k. Not just the ability to wait, but the ability to wait with a good attitude.

10l. Our lives are still giving forth a sweet aroma before the Lord.

10m. Something called godliness.

10n. Brotherly affection or kindness. True Christian love.

11a. Humility of Christ.

11b. Humility, meekness, kindness, and gentleness. Out into the world where we are to act like Jesus, giving forth a sweet-smelling aroma and having a soothing personality.

11c. The Kingdom.

12a. Not by our effort or strain or good works, but from knowing God personally and intimately.

12b. Sitting in the Presence of God and allowing Him to do a work on the inside.

12c. People who are willing to be changed from what they are to what only He can make them to be.

12d. The Lord will do the transforming and transfiguring of us — in His own way and in His own time — as we simply fellowship with Him in the inner man.

12e. It comes from abiding in the Lord and allowing Him to abide in you. It is His divine Presence that dissolves the hardness of your soul so that sweet-smelling fragrances pour forth from you.

12f. Learn to fellowship with Him so He can develop in you a soothing tongue and spirit.

Conclusion

1. The importance of how much blessing — and how much damage — we do by the words of our mouth.

2. Containers of power.

3. Empty; idle; vain; useless. God.

4. Return to Him after accomplishing His will and purpose.

5. It is out of the abundance of the heart that the mouth speaks — for good or for evil.

6. Words; declarations; judged.

7. So that what issues forth from them is not only truthful, but also kind and positive and edifying and in line with the will of God.

8. Your thoughts and words.

9. The help of the indwelling Spirit of God.

10. Attitude.

11. Submit yourself to the Lord and in humility ask Him to transform you into the image and nature of His Son Jesus Christ.

Endnotes

Chapter 1

[1] *Webster's II New College Dictionary* (Boston: Houghton Mifflin Company, 1995), s.v. "wisdom."

[2] Webster's, s.v. "prudent."

Chapter 2

[1] W. E. Vine, Merrill F. Unger, William White Jr., "New Testament Section," in *Vine's Complete Expository Dictionary of Old and New Testament Words* (Nashville: Thomas Nelson, Inc., 1984), p. 121, s.v. "CONFIRM, CONFIRMATION," A. Verbs, No. 1, *BEBAIOO.*

[2] Vine, A. Verbs, No. 3, *KUROO.*

[3] Vine, B. Noun, *BEBAIOSIS.*

Chapter 3

[1] James E. Strong, "Hebrew and Chaldee Dictionary," in *Strong's Exhaustive Concordance of the Bible* (Nashville: Abingdon, 1890), p. 32, entry #1897, s.v. "meditate," Joshua 1:8.

[2] Strong, "Hebrew," p. 115, entry #7878, s.v., "meditate," Psalm 119:148.

Chapter 7

[1] Webster's II, s.v. "bridle."

[2] Webster's II, s.v. "bit."

Chapter 10

[1] Vine, "New Testament Section," p. 580, s.v. "slanderer."

[2] James Strong, "Greek Dictionary of the New Testament," in *The New Strong's Exhaustive Concordance of the Bible* (Nashville: Thomas Nelson, Inc., 1990).

Chapter 12

[1] *Webster's New World Dictionary of the American Language* (New World Publishing Company, 1969), s.v. "busybody."

[2] Webster's II, s.v. "busybody."

[3] Webster's II, s.v. "gossip."

[4] Vine, "New Testament Section," p. 580, s.v. "slanderer."

[5] Webster's II, s.v. "slander."

[6] Webster's II, s.v. "whisper."

Chapter 13

[1] Webster's II, s.v. "disposition."

[2] Hannah Hurnard, *Mountains of Spices* (Wheaton: Tyndale House, Inc., 1979).

[3] Hurnard, pp. 222-229.

[4] Hurnard, pp. 168-174.

[5] Hurnard, pp. 136-144.

[6] Refers to relationship with God — the way man related to Him before Jesus came. In the Old Testament the outer court, inner court, and Holy of Holies were separate areas in the tabernacle. Under the Old Covenant, the tabernacle was the house of God, His dwelling place, the place of prayer for His people. (See Exodus 29:42,43.) Under the New Covenant, we believers are now God's house, His dwelling place, His temple (1 Corinthians 3:16); we can personally come into His throne room, into the Holy of Holies, which is His Presence, and we can have a personal relationship with Him.

About the Author

JOYCE MEYER has been teaching the Word of God since 1976 and in full-time ministry since 1980. She is the bestselling author of more than seventy inspirational books, including *Approval Addiction, In Pursuit of Peace, How to Hear from God,* and *Battlefield of the Mind.* She has also released thousands of audio teachings as well as a complete video library. Joyce's *Enjoying Everyday Life®* radio and television programs are broadcast around the world, and she travels extensively conducting conferences. Joyce and her husband, Dave, are the parents of four grown children and make their home in St. Louis, Missouri.

To contact the author write:
Joyce Meyer Ministries
P. O. Box 655
Fenton, Missouri 63026
or call: (636) 349-0303

Internet Address: www.joycemeyer.org

Please include your testimony or help received from this book when you write. Your prayer requests are welcome.

To contact the author
in Canada, please write:
Joyce Meyer Ministries Canada, Inc.
Lambeth Box 1300
London, ON N6P 1T5
or call: (636) 349-0303

In Australia, please write:
Joyce Meyer Ministries-Australia
Locked Bag 77
Mansfield Delivery Centre
Queensland 4122
or call: (07) 3349 1200

In England, please write:
Joyce Meyer Ministries
P. O. Box 1549
Windsor
SL4 1GT
or call: 01753 831102

Expect a Move of God in Your Life . . . Suddenly!

*Enjoying Where You Are on the Way to
Where You Are Going*

The Most Important Decision You Will Ever Make

When, God, When?

Why, God, Why?

The Word, the Name, the Blood

Tell Them I Love Them

Peace

The Root of Rejection

If Not for the Grace of God *

JOYCE MEYER SPANISH TITLES

*Las Siete Cosas Que Te Roban el Gozo
(Seven Things That Steal Your Joy)*

*Empezando Tu Día Bien
(Starting Your Day Right)*

BOOKS BY DAVE MEYER

Life Lines